SpringerBriefs in Law

SpringerBriefs present concise summaries of cutting-edge research and practical applications across a wide spectrum of fields. Featuring compact volumes of 50 to 125 pages, the series covers a range of content from professional to academic. Typical topics might include:

- A timely report of state-of-the art analytical techniques
- A bridge between new research results, as published in journal articles, and a contextual literature review
- A snapshot of a hot or emerging topic
- A presentation of core concepts that students must understand in order to make independent contributions

SpringerBriefs in Law showcase emerging theory, empirical research, and practical application in Law from a global author community. SpringerBriefs are characterized by fast, global electronic dissemination, standard publishing contracts, standardized manuscript preparation and formatting guidelines, and expedited production schedules.

Tomohiro Mikanagi

Toward Stronger Rule of Law Against Attempts to Acquire Territory by Force

A Practitioner's View

Springer

Tomohiro Mikanagi
Permanent Mission of Japan to the United Nations
New York, NY, USA

ISSN 2192-855X ISSN 2192-8568 (electronic)
SpringerBriefs in Law
ISBN 978-981-95-2813-4 ISBN 978-981-95-2814-1 (eBook)
https://doi.org/10.1007/978-981-95-2814-1

This Springer imprint is published by the registered company Springer Nature Singapore Pte Ltd.
The registered company address is: 152 Beach Road, #21-01/04 Gateway East, Singapore 189721, Singapore

I dedicate this book to my wife, the late Masami Mikanagi.

Contents

About the Author

Tomohiro Mikanagi is currently holding the position of Ambassador Extraordinary and Plenipotentiary, Deputy Permanent Representative of Japan to the United Nations. He also has the title of Ambassador-at-Large for Cooperation on International Law.

He studied international law at the University of Tokyo (BA) and University of Cambridge (Diploma and LL.M). He was also a visiting fellow at the Lauterpacht Centre for International Law in Cambridge. He has been publishing various articles on international law in a personal capacity, and this book is also written in this capacity.

In his diplomatic career, Ambassador Mikanagi has had extensive experience in the area of international law. He has served for more than ten years at the International Legal Affairs Bureau of the Japanese Ministry of Foreign Affairs, and held the titles of Deputy Director and Director of the International Legal Affairs Division, Deputy Legal Advisor and Legal Advisor. He has also served in London and Beijing as a diplomat.

Abbreviations

EEBC	Eritrea-Ethiopia Boundary Commission
EECC	Eritrea-Ethiopia Claims Commission
ESS	Emergency Special Session
ICJ	International Court of Justice
IDF	Israeli Defence Forces
ILC	International Law Commission
OAU	Organization of African Unity
OPT	Occupied Palestinian Territory
PATBF	prohibition of acquisition of territory by force
PCIJ	Permanent Court of International Justice
PUF	prohibition of use of force
TILS	Tokyo International Law Seminar
UN	United Nations
UNEF	United Nations Emergency Force
UNMEE	UN Mission in Ethiopia and Eritrea
VCLT	Vienna Convention on the Law of Treaties
(UN)GA	(United Nations) General Assembly

Chapter 1
Introduction and Overview

1.1 Aim of the Book

Efforts made since the early twentieth century to stop forcible territorial acquisition through the development of international law have been at the centre of the international community's pursuit of international peace and security. According to Brunk and Hakimi, who wrote a very timely article on the prohibition of acquisition of territory by force in the American Journal of International Law in 2024, 'research in political science shows that the desire to acquire territory has for centuries been a principal impetus for acts of military aggression', and 'numerous studies show that disputes over territory are more likely than other kinds of disputes to become violent'. They argue that 'to the extent that the prohibition of annexations reduces the prospects of acquiring territory through war, it likely also reduces the incentives to go to war'.[1]

On the other hand, even before the Russian invasion of Ukraine in 2022, it was apparent that the rule of law at the international level was still weak, especially when it comes to the issues relating to the use of force. Despite this weakness of the rule of law against use of force, until 2022, post-war efforts based on the United Nations (UN) Charter seemed to have succeeded in preventing outright attempts by nuclear-weapon States to acquire another sovereign State's internationally recognised territory by use of force.[2] Regrettably, this situation turned out to be a temporary success. Therefore, I believe that it is the right time to review the efforts made so far to stop forcible territorial acquisition and to examine the current state of rules of international law against attempts to acquire territory by force.

---

[1] Brunk and Hakimi (2024), p. 443.

[2] Brunk and Hakimi observed: 'Efforts to annex territory dropped precipitously after World War II and especially after the 1970s. On this particular prohibition, if on little else in the global security architecture, states broadly converged'. Ibid., p. 441.

T. Mikanagi, *Toward Stronger Rule of Law Against Attempts to Acquire Territory by Force*, SpringerBriefs in Law,
https://doi.org/10.1007/978-981-95-2814-1_1

To state the aim of this book in more detail, let me explain the title of the book. First, the meaning of the term 'rule of law' requires clarification. In the international community where enforcement and judicial mechanisms are much weaker than in national systems, the observance of law is difficult to ensure, especially when and where the use of force is involved. The late Professor Crawford examined the existence of the rule of law at the international level in his general course on public international law at the Hague Academy of International Law in 2013. In this lecture, he examined whether the international legal system can be considered to be governed by the rule of law, using the following five features as benchmarks: (i) equality under the law, (ii) democracy and accountability, (iii) no institution above the law, (iv) existence of constitution, and (v) absence of irremediable injustice in the society.[3] Professor Crawford's lecture examined the state of international community against these benchmarks and examined whether the rule of law exists at the international level.

In this small book, however, I am hoping to use the term 'rule of law' in a more flexible manner. Here, 'rule of law' does not necessarily mean a situation where the rules of international law are observed to a certain degree, but instead the power of international law in stopping attempts to acquire territory by force. The use of the term 'stronger' in the title indicates this meaning of 'rule of law'. 'Rule of law' consists of 'rule' and 'law'. 'Law' is international law, and, to strengthen the rule of law, relevant rules of international law must be clarified. 'Rule' is the controlling power which makes States observe the law. This power is exercised through enforcement mechanisms and judicial mechanisms in the national rule of law. In the international rule of law, as these mechanisms are weaker than the national systems, pressure from third States needs to play an important role. In the UN system, the enforcement mechanism consists mainly of the Security Council, and the judicial mechanism consists mainly of the International Court of Justice (ICJ). As a forum where third States express their views, the United Nations General Assembly (UNGA) is playing an increasingly important role.

Concerning relevant rules of international law 'against attempts to acquire territory by force', this book will examine the prohibition of use of force (hereinafter abbreviated as 'PUF') under Article 2(4) of the United Nations Charter and the prohibition of acquisition of territory by force (hereinafter abbreviated as 'PATBF'). These abbreviations may not look familiar to readers, but, as these terms appear very frequently in this book, please allow me to use these abbreviations to save space. Regarding PUF, Article 2(4) of the UN Charter provides as follows:

> All Members shall refrain in their international relations from the threat or use of force against the territorial integrity or political independence of any state, or in any other manner inconsistent with the Purposes of the United Nations.

PUF under Article 2(4) has become customary international law. Article 2(4) of the UN Charter does not directly refer to the acquisition of territory. The clear reference to PATBF was made in 1970 in the resolution 2625 (XXV) adopted by the UNGA

[3] Crawford (2013), pp. 342–343.

on 24 October 1970, entitled 'Declaration on Principles of International Law concerning Friendly Relations and Cooperation among States in accordance with the Charter of the United Nations' (hereinafter 'the Friendly Relations Declaration' or 'the 1970 Declaration').[4] This declaration provides:

> The territory of a State shall not be the object of military occupation resulting from the use of force in contravention of the provisions of the Charter. The territory of a State shall not be the object of acquisition by another State resulting from the threat or use of force. No territorial acquisition resulting from the threat or use of force shall be recognized as legal.

Finally, let me also explain what 'A Practitioner's View' means. As a book written by a former legal advisor working for a government, this book is based on an approach which is probably taken by many contemporary practitioners advising governments, which include legal advisors inside the governments and external counsels advising the governments. With the increasing amount of jurisprudence accumulated through the ICJ and other third-party dispute settlement bodies, practitioners working in the area of international law are increasingly relying on views expressed by these bodies. It is also important for them to make recommendations that can win support from other governments, and, for this legal diplomacy, persuasive narrative based on clear evidence and logic tends to be critically important. In this regard, in addition to the views expressed by third-party dispute settlement bodies, authoritative literature should be referred to, and States' views on legal matters expressed in resolutions adopted by the overwhelming majority in the UNGA and other relevant forums should also be respected. Furthermore, as a tool for legal diplomacy, possible utilisation of legal mechanisms, including advisory proceedings, should be kept in their mind in formulating advice.

1.2 Relevant Events: 2022–2024

The period between 2022 and 2024 saw many events relating to attempts to acquire territory by force. As essential background to this book, these events will be briefly reviewed below. My thoughts on these events are naturally affected by my own experience, and, as a matter of transparency, please allow me to mention where I was in this period. From 2022 to 2024, I was Legal Advisor of the Japanese Ministry of Foreign Affairs and participated in discussions on the events mentioned below. From October 2024, I moved to NY as Deputy Permanent Representative to the UN and attended Security Council meetings in the last quarter of 2024. Japan was a non-permanent member of the Security Council from 2023 to 2024 and the President of G7 in 2023.

24 February 2022 Russia started invasion of Ukraine.

2 March 2022 GA resolution ES-11/1 was adopted with 141 voting in favour, 5 against, and 35 abstentions. This resolution, which was titled 'Aggression against

[4] UN Doc. A/RES/2625 (XXV).

Ukraine', reaffirmed the GA's commitment to the sovereignty, independence, unity and territorial integrity of Ukraine within its internationally recognised borders and deplored in the strongest terms the aggression by Russia against Ukraine in violation of Article 2 (4) of the Charter.

23–27 September 2022 Russia conducted so-called 'referendums' on the annexation of the Donetsk, Kherson, Luhansk and Zaporizhzhia regions of Ukraine.

12 October 2022 GA resolution ES-11/4 titled 'Territorial integrity of Ukraine: defending the principles of the Charter of the United Nations' was adopted with 143 voting in favour, 5 against and 35 abstaining. This resolution declared Russia's attempted annexation as illegal and invalid. Resolution ES-11/4 reads as follows:

> The General Assembly, …
>
> Reaffirming the principle of customary international law, as restated in its resolution 2625 (XXV) of 24 October 1970, entitled "Declaration on Principles of International Law concerning Friendly Relations and Cooperation among States in accordance with the Charter of the United Nations", that no territorial acquisition resulting from the threat or use of force shall be recognized as legal, …
>
> 2. Condemns the organization by the Russian Federation of illegal so-called referendums in regions within the internationally recognized borders of Ukraine and the attempted illegal annexation of the Donetsk, Kherson, Luhansk and Zaporizhzhia regions of Ukraine, following the organization of the above-mentioned referendums;
>
> 3. Declares that the unlawful actions of the Russian Federation with regard to the illegal so-called referendums held from 23 to 27 September 2022 in parts of the Donetsk, Kherson, Luhansk and Zaporizhzhia regions of Ukraine that, in part, are or have been under the temporary military control of the Russian Federation, and the subsequent attempted illegal annexation of these regions, have no validity under international law and do not form the basis for any alteration of the status of these regions of Ukraine;
>
> 4. Calls upon all States, international organizations and United Nations specialized agencies not to recognize any alteration by the Russian Federation of the status of any or all of the Donetsk, Kherson, Luhansk or Zaporizhzhia regions of Ukraine, and to refrain from any action or dealing that might be interpreted as recognizing any such altered status; …

30 December 2022 GA adopted resolution 77/247 requesting the ICJ to render an advisory opinion relating to the Occupied Palestinian Territory (OPT).

12 January 2023 Japan, as the President of the Security Council in January 2023, hosted an open debate of the Council on the 'Rule of Law among Nations'.[5] Seventy-seven Member States made statements, and most of them emphasised the importance of the rule of law.

18 April 2023 G7 foreign ministers issued Communiqué in Karuizawa, Japan.[6] It strongly opposed 'any unilateral attempts to change the peacefully established status of territories by force or coercion anywhere in the world'.

20 May 2023 G7 leaders issued Communiqué in Hiroshima, Japan, also expressing strong opposition to 'any unilateral attempts to change the peacefully

---

[5] See the concept note for the ministerial-level open debate of the Security Council on the theme 'The promotion and strengthening of the rule of law in the maintenance of international peace and security: the rule of law among nations' (S/2023/1).

[6] G7 Foreign Ministers' Communiqué, 18 April 2023, Karuizawa, Nagano, Japan, available at https://www.mofa.go.jp/files/100492731.pdf

established status of territories by force or coercion anywhere in the world' and reaffirmed that the acquisition of territory by force is prohibited.[7]

7 October 2023 Many legal issues arose from the situation after Hamas's attack on Israel on 7 October 2023.

19–26 February 2024 The oral proceedings for the advisory opinion on the legal issues relating to the OPT were held at the ICJ; 49 States and 3 international organisations participated.[8]

19 July 2024 The ICJ rendered Advisory Opinion on 'Legal Consequences arising from the Policies and Practices of Israel in the Occupied Palestinian Territory, including East Jerusalem' (the 2024 ICJ Advisory Opinion). The ICJ found, *inter alia*, that 'to seek to acquire sovereignty over an occupied territory, as shown by the policies and practices adopted by Israel in East Jerusalem and the West Bank, is contrary to the prohibition of the use of force in international relations and its corollary principle of the non-acquisition of territory by force'.[9]

22 September 2024 At 'the Summit of the Future' held in the UNGA, world leaders adopted a document titled 'the Pact for the Future'.[10] The Pact for the Future referred to the rule of law at the international level and the 1970 Declaration. The relevant part of the Pact reads as follows:

> **II. International peace and security**
>
> 32. The global security landscape is undergoing profound transformation. We are concerned about the increasing and diverse threats to international peace and security, particularly violations of the purposes and principles of the Charter, and the growing risks of a nuclear war which could pose an existential threat to humanity. Amid this changing context, we remain committed to establish a just and lasting peace. We reaffirm our commitment to act in accordance with international law, including the Charter and its purposes and principles, and to fulfil our obligations in good faith. We reaffirm the imperative of upholding and promoting the rule of law at the international level in accordance with the principles of the Charter of the United Nations, and in this regard recall the importance of the Declaration on Principles of International Law concerning Friendly Relations and Cooperation among States in accordance with the Charter of the United Nations (Resolution 2625 (XXV)).

The basic stance of Japan in this period is summarised in the following statement made by Prime Minister Kishida at the UNGA on 20 September 2022:

> We stand at a historic watershed moment. … It is an imperative to maintain the international order where the rule of law is firmly established. … What is crucial is for any and all countries to be under the rule of law – not the rule by force, which we absolutely cannot allow. … Especially at a time when the existing international order is being tested around the world,

---

[7] G7 Hiroshima Leaders' Communiqué, 20 May 2023, available at https://www.mofa.go.jp/files/100506878.pdf

[8] The author made an oral statement as the Agent of Japan, focusing on the application of PATBF, together with Professor Dapo Akande of Oxford University.

[9] Legal Consequences arising from the Policies and Practices of Israel in the Occupied Palestinian Territory, including East Jerusalem, Advisory Opinion, 19 July 2024 [hereinafter cited as the 2024 ICJ Advisory Opinion], para. 179.

[10] UN Doc. A/RES/79/1. https://www.un.org/sites/un2.un.org/files/sotf-co-facilitators-zero-draft_pact-for-the-future.pdf

> now is the time to return to the vision and principles of the UN Charter and mobilize our strength and wisdom to ensure an international order based on the rule of law. … We need to remind ourselves that the rule of law is especially important for vulnerable nations. … The following basic principles for States emerge from this declaration: first, break away from 'rule by force' and pursue 'rule of law' through observing international law in good faith; second, in this regard, do not allow any attempts to change the status quo of territories and areas by force or coercion; and third, to cooperate with one another against serious violations of the principles of the UN Charter.

My interest in the legal issues relating to attempts to acquire territory by force started earlier than 2022. The Russian attempt to 'annex' Crimea in 2014 and the ICJ judgment on the Costa Rica v Nicaragua case in 2015[11] were among the events which made me think about relevant rules of international law. Based on my earlier thoughts on these events, I wrote a short article in 2018.[12] In this article, I examined the application of Article 2(3) and (4) of the UN Charter to the establishment of a military presence in a disputed territory. My research for this article brought my attention to the ICJ's Advisory Opinion on 'Legal Consequences of the Construction of a Wall in the Occupied Palestinian Territory' in 2004 (the 2004 ICJ Wall Advisory Opinion).[13] This Advisory Opinion found that PATBF is 'a corollary' of PUF under Article 2(4) of the UN Charter, but it stopped short of making determination on the application of PATBF to the OPT, and the ICJ's Advisory Opinion of 19 July 2024 mentioned above was the first time the ICJ applied PATBF and found its violation.

1.3 Overview of the Book

This book will review efforts made in the international community to stop forcible territorial acquisition through the development of international law and examine the current state of the rules of international law relating to the attempts to acquire territory by force.

Chapter 2 will review the history of efforts since the early twentieth century to stop forcible territorial acquisition through the development of law and intergovernmental mechanisms. There are already several important publications on the history of PATBF, and the aim of Chap. 2 is limited to providing historical context to the discussion in the following chapters and identifying inherent difficulty in outlawing forcible territorial acquisition which derives from the reality of the world.

Chapters 3 and 4 will examine the scope (Chap. 3) and effect (Chap. 4) of the relevant rules of international law. As is indicated by the fact that the 2024 ICJ Advisory Opinion was the first case where the ICJ applied PATBF, the discussion on PATBF does not seem to have reached its high level of maturity. The detailed

[11] See Sects. 3.3.1 and 3.4.3 below.

[12] Mikanagi (2018).

[13] Legal Consequences of the Construction of a Wall in the Occupied Palestinian Territory, Advisory Opinion, 9 July 2004, ICJ Rep. (2004) [hereinafter cited as the 2004 Wall Advisory Opinion].

contents of PATBF and its relationship with PUF have not yet been fully clarified by international courts and tribunal nor by academic writings. However, to strengthen the rule of law, the relevant rules of international law must be clarified. Practitioners advising governments are expected to give the best possible advice based on currently available evidence, and these chapters will endeavour to do so. As will be explained in Sect. 3.2, the examination in Chaps. 3 and 4 will be mainly based on GA resolutions, including the 1970 Friendly Relations Declaration, views of international courts and tribunals, and academic literature.

In Chap. 3, at the outset, typical images of attempts to acquire territory by force will be presented for the following discussion on legal issues in Chaps. 3 and 4. Section 3.1 will preliminarily examine the relationship between PUF and PATBF, and Sects. 3.3 and 3.4 will analyse elements contributing to the violation of PUF and PATBF. Section 3.3 will examine various contexts in which attempts are made to acquire territory by force, and Sect. 3.4 will examine elements of acts constituting such attempts. Based on the analysis in these sections, Sect. 3.5 will explore hypothetical cases where PUF and PATBF are likely to be violated. In cases where PATBF is difficult to apply and PUF is easier to apply, PUF may work as an alternative rule of international law against potential attempts to acquire territory by force. Therefore, in Chap. 3, the application of PUF will be examined alongside the examination of PATBF. The analysis in Chap. 3 relies on currently available evidence and plausible logic. Therefore, arguments made there are sometimes inevitably rather inconclusive, but it is hoped that they stimulate further thoughts and discussions by readers.

In Chap. 4, first, Sect. 4.1 will examine PATBF's effect in denying the acquisition of territorial title through use of force in self-defence. Section 4.2 will look at PATBF's effect upon third States based on the 2024 Advisory Opinion. The Stimson Doctrine, which will be discussed in Sect. 2.1.2, was a doctrine demanding third States not to recognise the acquisition of territory by unlawful use of force, but the 2024 Advisory Opinion mentioned obligations for third States which are broader than non-recognition.

In Chaps. 3 and 4, after legal examination of the scope and effect of the relevant rules of international law, some policy suggestions for strengthening the rule of law against attempts to acquire territory by force will also be made in Sects. 3.4 and 4.2.6.

The final chapter, Chap. 5, will ask whether we have made progress in the past 100 years in strengthening the rule of law against attempts to acquire territory by force, and think about what we can do now.

As I have been working as an official of the Japanese government for many years, my thoughts are inevitably influenced by my experience as an official of Japan. At the same time, as an official serving in the legal department for many years, my opinion might have also influenced the Japanese government's position to some extent. In any event, I have been writing academic articles on international law in a personal capacity for many years, and the contents of this book reflect my own personal opinion and not the official position of the Japanese government.

References

Brunk, I., & Hakimi, M. (2024). The Prohibition of Annexations and the Foundations of Modern International Law, AJIL 118(3): 417–467

Crawford, James. (2013). *Chance, Order, Change: The Course of International Law*, Pocketbooks of the Hague Academy of International Law (Recueil des Cours 365: 13–390)

Mikanagi, T. (2018). Establishing a Military Presence in a Disputed Territory: Interpretation of Article 2(3) and (4) of the UN Charter, ICLQ 67(4): 1021–1034

Chapter 2
Efforts Against Forcible Territorial Acquisition Since 1919

2.1 Efforts and Failure in the Inter-War Period

2.1.1 League of Nations and Kellogg-Briand Pact

In the nineteenth century, the acquisition of territory by 'conquest' followed by an annexation, which was called 'subjugation', was allowed under international law.[1] According to Korman, in 1917, both the Russian Provisional Government after the Russian Revolution and US President Wilson started to argue against annexation, and on 8 January 1918, President Wilson announced the Fourteen Points as a basis for an acceptable peace after World War I.[2] The Fourteen Points denied acquisition of territory through conquest secretly agreed among States during World War I. The first two sentences of the Fourteen Points read as follows:

> It will be our wish and purpose that the processes of peace, when they are begun, shall be absolutely open and that they shall involve and permit henceforth no secret understandings of any kind. The day of conquest and aggrandizement is gone by; so is also the day of secret covenants entered into in the interest of particular governments and likely at some unlooked-for moment to upset the peace of the world.

The Treaty of Versailles ending World War I was signed in Paris on 28 June 1919, and the Covenant of the League of Nations was integrated into the Treaty. Article 10 of the Covenant refereed to the aggression against the territorial integrity of Members of the League. The article provided:

---

[1] Jennings and Watts (1992), p. 698, Shaw (1991), p. 287, Akehurst (1987), p. 148, Clapham (2012), p. 176.

[2] Korman (1996), pp. 135–138. For the Fourteen Points, see US National Archive <https://www.archives.gov/milestone-documents/president-woodrow-wilsons-14-points>.

T. Mikanagi, *Toward Stronger Rule of Law Against Attempts to Acquire Territory by Force*, SpringerBriefs in Law,
https://doi.org/10.1007/978-981-95-2814-1_2

> The Members of the League undertake to respect and preserve as against external aggression the territorial integrity and existing political independence of all Members of the League. In case of any such aggression or in case of any threat or danger of such aggression the Council shall advise upon the means by which this obligation shall be fulfilled.

Therefore, the acquisition of territory through aggression against other Members' territorial integrity was against Article 10 of the Covenant. On 27 August 1928, the General Treaty for the Renunciation of War as an Instrument of National Policy, which is also known as the Kellogg-Briand Pact or the Pact of Paris, was signed at Paris. Article 1 of the Kellogg-Briand Pact provided:

> The High Contracting Parties solemnly declare in the names of their respective peoples that they condemn recourse to war for the solution of international controversies, and renounce it, as an instrument of national policy in their relations with one another.

This Pact renounced the recourse to war as an instrument of national policy, and, according to Korman, the acquisition of territory through war which had been started as an instrument of national policy was, in principle, prohibited under the Pact.[3]

2.1.2 'Manchurian Incident' and the Stimson Doctrine[4]

On 18 September 1931, the 'Manchurian Incident' occurred, and Japan declared the establishment of the 'new State of Manchukuo'. On 7 January 1932, US Secretary of State Henry Stimson sent similar notes to China and Japan. In these notes, the American Government notified that it would not recognise any situation, treaty, or agreement which might be brought about by means contrary to the Kellogg-Briand Pact. The relevant part of the notes reads as follows:[5]

> [T]he American Government deems it to be its duty to notify both the Imperial Japanese Government and the Government of the Chinese Republic that it cannot admit the legality of any situation de facto nor does it intend to recognize any treaty or agreement entered into between those Governments, or agents thereof, which may impair the treaty rights of the United States or its citizens in China, including those that relate to the sovereignty, the independence, or the territorial and administrative integrity of the Republic of China, or to the international policy relative to China, commonly known as the open door policy; and that it does not intend to recognize any situation, treaty, or agreement which may be brought about by means contrary to the covenants and obligations of the Pact of Paris of August 27th, 1928, to which treaty both China and Japan as well as the United States are parties.

The content of these notes became known as the principle of non-recognition, or the Stimson Doctrine. This doctrine was based on the principle that an illegal act cannot

[3] There were exceptions to this prohibition. See Korman (1996), p. 197.

[4] For development of the prohibition of acquisition of territory by force and the principle of non-recognition in Latin America, which started earlier than 1931, see Brunk and Hakimi (2024), p. 426, Korman (1996), pp. 234–238, 240–242.

[5] Wright (1932), p. 342.

give birth to a right in law (*ex injuria jus non oritur*). If a State tried to acquire a new territory through acts prohibited under the Kellogg-Briand Pact, the unlawful act could not create lawful territorial title. This principle of non-recognition had the effect of exerting pressure on States not to attempt to acquire territory through war prohibited under the Kellogg-Briand Pact.[6]

In 1963, Ian Brownlie examined the application of this principle to events took place between 1928 and 1945 in his book 'International Law and the Use of Force by States'. The practice of States in this period was not very consistent, but according to Brownlie: 'The British *de jure* recognition of Italian sovereignty over Ethiopia and the Munich Agreement were the most significant instances of failure to observe legal standards but the predominant trend in state practice was in favour of non-recognition'.[7]

2.1.3 Inherent Difficulty in Outlawing Acquisition of Territory by Force

Despite Brownlie's observation on the 'predominant trend in state practice', this State practice did not stop States with ambition acquiring territory by force, and, with hindsight, only the all-out war against the Axis Powers could stop them. E. H. Carr's book 'The Twenty Years' Crisis, 1919–1939', which critically analysed the situation in the inter-war period in 1939, pointed out:[8]

> The utopian assumption that there is a world interest in peace which is identifiable with the interest of each individual nation helped politicians and political writers everywhere to evade the unpalatable fact of a fundamental divergence of interest between nations desirous of maintaining the *status quo* and nations desirous of changing it.

What Carr mentioned as the 'utopian assumption' here was the assumption that international legal mechanisms under the Covenant of the League of Nations and the Kellogg-Briand Pact would be able to defend the new *status quo* created by the Versailles Treaty against nations desirous of changing it. In other words, it was the belief that the rule of law would protect the new *status quo* without resorting to force. According to Carr, there was a broad agreement on the need for adjustment in the provisions of the Versailles Treaty protecting the new *status quo*. He wrote:[9]

> The mass of political opinion in Great Britain and Germany (and in most other countries) agreed for many years that a creation of justice and injustice could properly be applied to the Versailles Treaty; and there was a surprisingly considerable, though far from complete, consensus of opinion about the parts of it which were just and unjust respectively.

---

[6] Korman (1996), pp. 238–240.

[7] Brownlie (1963), p. 420.

[8] Carr (1939), pp. 51, 78, 201, See also Koskenniemi (2001), p. 181, Korman (1996), pp. 242–243.

[9] Carr (1939), p. 201.

Carr was talking about Germany. The strong feeling of dissatisfaction about the new territorial *status quo* seems to have been an important element in Germany's resistance to the emerging rules outlawing acquisition of territory by force. Carr referred to the occupation of the Rhineland as an example.[10] Korman also refers to the occupation of the Rhineland as a compromise between the principle of non-annexation and French demand for security.[11] According to Korman, Article 10 of the Covenant of the League of Nations was widely understood to prevent all territorial changes imposed by force.[12] However, the changes of frontier after WWI seem to have sown the seeds of future conflicts.

Regarding Japan, Professor Masaharu Yanagihara explains Japan's attitude toward modern European international law from the latter half of nineteenth century to the first half of the twentieth century in three phases: 'The age of civilization and enlightenment' from 1853 to 1905, 'the age of pseudo-equality' from 1905 to 1931, and 'the age of militarism' from 1931 to 1945.[13] His Hague Academy lecture in 2015 explains:

> … when Japan began to be under the impression that it was regarded as a Western-styled civilized State, Japan began to entertain strong suspicions about sovereign equality among civilized States. … In the third stage of the age of militarism, from 1931 to 1945 Japan could not follow up a fairly drastic change of international law, especially 'outlawry of war' or prohibition of aggressive war, and could not understand, or did not want to understand, the real meaning of the 1928 Briand-Kellogg Pact. There was without any doubt lack of sensitivity to changes in international law.

In Japan's case, the feeling of dissatisfaction about the contemporary state of the world weakened its efforts to keep up with the emerging rules outlawing acquisition of territory by force. Looking back at this period, in 2015, then Japanese Prime Minister, the late Mr. Shinzo Abe, stated in his speech marking the 70th anniversary of the end of the war as follows:

> After World War I, which embroiled the world, the movement for self-determination gained momentum and put brakes on colonization that had been underway. It was a horrible war that claimed as many as ten million lives. With a strong desire for peace stirred in them, people founded the League of Nations and brought forth the General Treaty for Renunciation of War. There emerged in the international community a new tide of outlawing war itself.
>
> At the beginning, Japan, too, kept steps with other nations. However, with the Great Depression setting in and the Western countries launching economic blocs by involving colonial economies, Japan's economy suffered a major blow. In such circumstances, Japan's sense of isolation deepened and it attempted to overcome its diplomatic and economic deadlock through the use of force. Its domestic political system could not serve as a brake to stop such attempts. In this way, Japan lost sight of the overall trends in the world.
>
> With the 'Manchurian Incident', followed by the withdrawal from the League of Nations, Japan gradually transformed itself into a challenger to the new international order

---

[10] Carr (1939), p. 201.

[11] Korman (1996), p. 148.

[12] Korman (1996), pp. 187, 190–191.

[13] Yanagihara (2015), p. 348.

> that the international community sought to establish after tremendous sacrifices. Japan took the wrong course and advanced along the road to war.
>
> And, seventy years ago, Japan was defeated.

Thus, Japan learned a hard lesson from its own experience.

The League of Nations was weakened by the United States' failure to join it. For Germany, the new *status quo* created after WWI and protected by the legal system was not acceptable and the League could not effectively react to the challenges posed by Germany. Germany withdrew from the League in 1933 and dismissed the law protecting the *status quo* as unjust.[14] In the case of Japan, Japan tried to rely on the ambiguity of the newly developed international law but did not succeed, and Japan withdrew from the League in 1933. Thus, the efforts to stop forcible territorial acquisition through legal mechanisms established in the inter-war period failed.

These examples indicate difficulty in ensuring the compliance of rules outlawing acquisition of territory by force. This difficulty is partly due to the absence of universally acceptable territorial *status quo*. The dissatisfaction of States with territorial *status quo*, coupled with their disregard for international law, are causes of attempts to acquire territory by force. It is also partly due to the weakness of the international mechanism caused by the unwillingness of major powers in sacrificing their own interests for the effectiveness of collective security mechanisms. When some States, especially powerful States, are not satisfied with the existing territorial *status quo* and major powers do not give up their own interests for the effectiveness of collective security mechanism, there would be inherent difficulty in strengthening the rule of law against attempts to acquire territory by force.

2.2 Post-War Efforts to Overcome the Inherent Difficulty

2.2.1 United Nations Charter and the Role of the Security Council

As mentioned above, Article 2(4) of the United Nations Character prohibited the use of force as follows:

> All Members shall refrain in their international relations from the threat or use of force against the territorial integrity or political independence of any state, or in any other manner inconsistent with the Purposes of the United Nations.

The United Nations Charter established an enforcement mechanism in its Chapter VII. This system was designed to rely on the Security Council, which has the primary responsibility for the maintenance of international peace and security under Article 24 of the Charter. If attempts to acquire territory by force pose a threat to international peace and security, the Council has the primary responsibility to stop

[14] Koskenniemi (2001), pp. 236–238, pp. 261–265.

them through measures taken under Chapter VII. If the Council takes effective action to stop them, PUF and PATBF can be upheld through enforcement action under the UN Charter. However, the veto power of the permanent members of the Security Council (P5) restricts the ability of the Council to act against attempts to acquire territory by force, in cases where such an attempt is made by a P5 State or by a State in close relationship with one or more P5 States.

The only one case in UN history where the Council acted to take effective enforcement measures under Chapter VII against an attempt by a State to acquire territory by force was its response to Iraq in 1990. On 2 August 1990, when Iraq invaded Kuwait, the Council adopted resolution 660, which reads as follows:

> The Security Council,
> Alarmed by the invasion of Kuwait on 2 August 1990 by the military forces of Iraq,
> Determining that there exists a breach of international peace and security as regards the Iraqi invasion of Kuwait,
> Acting under Articles 39 and 40 of the Charter of the United Nations,
> 1. Condemns the Iraqi invasion of Kuwait;
> 2. Demands that Iraq withdraw immediately and unconditionally all its forces to the positions in which they were located on 1 August 1990; …

On 29 November 1990, the Council adopted resolution 678 and authorised Member States to use ‘all necessary means’, which included use of force, to uphold and implement resolution 660. Resolution 678 reads as follows:

> The Security Council, …
> Acting under Chapter VII of the Charter, …
> 2. Authorizes Member States co-operating with the Government of Kuwait, unless Iraq on or before 15 January 1991 fully implements, as set forth in paragraph 1 above, the above-mentioned resolutions, to use all necessary means to uphold and implement resolution 660 (1990) and all subsequent relevant resolutions and to restore international peace and security in the area; …

Under Chapter VII, the Council was expected to take military measures under Article 42, and Article 43 referred to special agreements between the Council and Member States for contributing military forces to be used for military actions under Article 42. The special agreements mentioned in Article 43 have not been signed and these provisions did not function as envisaged. Resolution 678 did not mention Article 42 and simply referred to Chapter VII.

The legal basis for this resolution was controversial at the time of adoption. Some writers interpreted this resolution as an endorsement of the right of collective self-defence.[15] Others argued that this resolution was based on Article 42 or Chapter VII as a whole.[16] The ‘Agenda for Peace’, a report by UN Secretary-General Boutros Boutros-Ghali in 1992, responding to a request by the Council for ‘analysis and recommendations’ to strengthen peacemaking and peace-keeping, did not categorise the action against Iraq in 1991 as Article 42 action and simply said: ‘In the

[15] Rostow (1991), p. 509. Weston (1991), pp. 518–522.

[16] Greenwood (1992), pp. 175–177, Gray (2018), pp. 273–274.

situation between Iraq and Kuwait, the Council chose to authorise Member States to take measures on its behalf'.[17]

This resolution was followed by other resolutions authorising the use of force by Member States.[18] In the case of the Iraqi invasion of Kuwait in 1990, despite the controversy over the precise legal basis, the Council acted against the Iraqi attempt to acquire territory by force. While there was disagreement over whether resolution 678 was based on the Council's authority under Chapter VII of the Charter or the Member States' right to collective self-defence, the military operation against Iraq in 1991, which was implemented in accordance with resolution 678, was widely accepted as lawful among the UN Member States and, in this case, the rule of law against an attempt to acquire territory by force seemed to function through lawful measures taken in accordance with resolutions adopted by the Council.

2.2.2 *Efforts through the General Assembly*

2.2.2.1 Clarification of Law by the Friendly Relations Declaration

Article 2(4) of the UN Charter clearly prohibited the use of force, but it did not directly refer to the acquisition of territory by force.[19] In the discussion on the situation in the Middle East, Security Council Resolution 242 adopted on 22 November 1967 referred to the inadmissibility of the acquisition of territory by war, but the clear enunciation on PATBF by the United Nations had to wait until 24 October 1970 when resolution 2625 (XXV) was adopted by the GA. This resolution was accompanied by the Friendly Relations Declaration.[20]

The preamble of the 1970 Declaration also referred to the importance of the UN Charter in the promotion of 'the rule of law among nations'. This was probably the first time when major UN documents on international law mentioned the rule of law at the international level. It also declared that the observance of the principles in the declaration is of the greatest importance for the maintenance of international peace and security. The relevant part of the preamble of the declaration reads:

> Bearing in mind also the paramount importance of the Charter of the United Nations in the promotion of the rule of law among nations, …
>
> Considering that the faithful observance of the principles of international law concerning friendly relations and co-operation among States and the fulfillment in good faith of the obligations assumed by States, in accordance with the Charter, is of the greatest importance

---

[17] Boutros Boutros-Ghali, An agenda for peace: preventive diplomacy, peacemaking and peace-keeping: report of the Secretary-General pursuant to the statement adopted by the Summit Meeting of the Security Council on 31 January 1992, para. 42. https://digitallibrary.un.org/record/145749?v=pdf

[18] De Wet (2024), p. 1703.

[19] For the situation between 1945 and 1970, including the discussion at the International Law Commission (ILC), see Brunk and Hakimi (2024), p. 434.

[20] UN Doc. A/RES/2625 (XXV).

> for the maintenance of international peace and security and for the implementation of the other purposes of the United Nations, ...

As mentioned in Chap. 1 above, this declaration provides:

> The territory of a State shall not be the object of military occupation resulting from the use of force in contravention of the provisions of the Charter. The territory of a State shall not be the object of acquisition by another State resulting from the threat or use of force. No territorial acquisition resulting from the threat or use of force shall be recognized as legal.

The 1970 Declaration contributes to the rule of law against attempts to acquire territory by force through the clarification of the existence of PATBF and its effect of imposing obligation upon third States.

In 1951, in his book titled 'American Diplomacy 1900–1950', George F. Kennan wrote: 'the idea of subordination of a large number of states to an international juridical regime, limiting their possibilities for aggression and injury to other states, implies that these are all states like our own, reasonably content with their international borders and status, at least to the extent that they would be willing to refrain from pressing for change without international agreement'. He observed that '[a]ctually, this has generally been true only of a portion of international society'.[21]

As explained above, the dissatisfaction about territorial *status quo* constituted the inherent difficulty in outlawing acquisition of territory by force in the inter-war period. By adopting the paragraph quoted above by consensus the 1970 Declaration seems to implicitly indicate that in 1970 the UN Member States generally preferred to maintain territorial *status quo*.[22] This attitude itself seems to be a remarkable change from what Kennan wrote in 1951.

The territorial situations in the world have changed since 1970, especially in the former Soviet Union. However, the changes in the territorial situations in the former Soviet Union were not made through use of force, and, if there is any dissatisfaction about territorial changes brought about without use of force after 1970, it should not justify violation of PATBF which was accepted in 1970.

2.2.2.2 Carefully Considered Opinions Expressed in GA Resolutions

When the Security Council fails to act against attempts to acquire territory by force due to veto by one or more P5 members, alternative ways to uphold the rule of law against such attempts must be explored. As an example of such attempts, the 'Uniting for Peace' procedure was created by GA resolution 377(V) adopted on 3 November 1950. This resolution:[23]

> 1. *Resolves* that if the Security Council, because of lack of unanimity of the permanent members, fails to exercise its primary responsibility for the maintenance of international peace and security in any case where there appears to be a threat to the peace, breach of the

---

[21] Kennan (1951), p. 103.

[22] Brunk and Hakimi (2024), p. 438.

[23] UN.Doc. A/RES/337(V).

> peace, or act of aggression, the General Assembly shall consider the matter immediately with a view to making appropriate recommendations to Members for collective measures, including in the case of a breach of the peace or act of aggression the use of armed force when necessary, to maintain or restore international peace and security. If not in session at the time, the General Assembly may meet in emergency special session within twenty-four hours of the request therefor. Such emergency special session shall be called if requested by the Security Council on the vote of any seven members,[24] or by a majority of the Members of the United Nations;

This procedure was utilised in 1956 to establish UN peacekeeping force 'UN Emergency Force (UNEF)' to supervise the cease-fire after the Suez Crisis. The first Emergency Special Session (ESS) of the GA was convened on 1 November 1956. In the following days several resolutions were adopted by the GA and UNEF was established.

On the other hand, Article 11(2) of the UN Charter provides:

> The General Assembly may discuss any questions relating to the maintenance of international peace and security brought before it by any Member of the United Nations, or by the Security Council, or by a state which is not a Member of the United Nations in accordance with Article 35, paragraph 2, and, except as provided in Article 12, may make recommendations with regard to any such questions to the state or states concerned or to the Security Council or to both. Any such question on which action is necessary shall be referred to the Security Council by the General Assembly either before or after discussion.

The last sentence of Article 11(2) prevents the GA from making recommendations on 'action'. The ICJ interpreted this 'action' to be enforcement action under Chapter VII.[25] Therefore, according to the ICJ's interpretation, the GA cannot make recommendation on enforcement measures which only the Security Council can take under Chapter VII. The legal effects of a GA resolution adopted in ESS under the Uniting for Peace procedure and a GA resolution adopted in an ordinary session are not different, but the fact that ESS is initiated by the Security Council may give additional weight to the resolutions adopted in ESSs.

As mentioned earlier, the GA adopted resolutions at the 11th ESS, including GA resolution ES-11/1 adopted on 2 March 2022,[26] deploring in the strongest terms the aggression by Russia against Ukraine in violation of Article 2 (4) of the UN Charter, and GA resolution ES-11/4 adopted on 12 October 2022,[27] condemning the attempted illegal annexation of the Donetsk, Kherson, Luhansk and Zaporizhzhia regions of Ukraine.

For UN Member States, GA resolutions sometimes put them in a difficult position to make a politically difficult choice, especially when they are under heavy diplomatic pressure from different sides, and they have to take a position on questions of a critical nature which might determine the direction of the development of

---

[24] This number was later amended to nine following the expansion of the Security Council in 1963.

[25] Certain Expenses of the United Nations (Article 17, paragraph 2, of the Charter), Advisory Opinion, 20 July 1962, ICJ Rep. 1962, pp. 164–165.

[26] UN Doc. A/RES/ESS-11/1.

[27] UN Doc. A/RES/ESS-11/4.

international law. GA resolutions are not legally binding, but, because of this difficulty, the resolutions on important legal issues adopted by a large majority of Member States, which have gone through careful consideration of the legal issues involved under difficult political circumstances, are likely to carry significant weight as the expression of their considered opinions.

2.2.3 *The Role of the International Court of Justice*

The Permanent Court of International Justice (PCIJ), which was established under Article 14 of the Covenant of the League of Nations, was succeeded by the International Court of Justice (ICJ). The ICJ is given the status of the principal judicial organ of the UN under Article 92 of the UN Charter. However, its jurisdictional basis remained like the system adopted under the PCIJ, which is based on the consents of States. Even now, only 74 out of 193 UN Member States are depositing declarations to accept the ICJ's jurisdiction under Article 36(2) of the ICJ Statute, and, even among the 74 States, many declarations have reservations excluding the issues relating to territory and/or use of force from the jurisdiction of the ICJ.[28]

In the absence of jurisdiction based on the declaration under Article 36(2) of the ICJ Statute or an international agreement providing for the jurisdiction, the utility of the advisory procedure of the ICJ has increasingly been explored by the UN Member States. On 8 December 2003, under the 'Uniting for Peace' mechanism, at its tenth ESS, the GA adopted resolution ES-10/14 to request the ICJ for an advisory opinion on the following question:[29]

> What are the legal consequences arising from the construction of the wall being built by Israel, the occupying Power, in the Occupied Palestinian Territory, including in and around East Jerusalem, as described in the Report of the Secretary-General, considering the rules and principles of international law, including the Fourth Geneva Convention of 1949, and relevant Security Council and General Assembly resolutions?

In response, the ICJ rendered its Advisory Opinion on 9 July 2004. In this 2004 ICJ Wall Advisory Opinion, the ICJ did not make determination on the PATBF. However, the ICJ, referring to the 1970 Declaration, said that PATBF is a 'corollary' of Article 2(4) of the UN Charter. The relevant part of the Opinion reads:[30]

> 87. The Court first recalls that, pursuant to Article 2, paragraph 4, of the United Nations Charter: "All Members shall refrain in their international relations from the threat or use of force against the territorial integrity or political independence of any State, or in any other manner inconsistent with the Purposes of the United Nations." On 24 October 1970, the General Assembly adopted resolution 2625 (XXV), entitled "Declaration on Principles of International Law concerning Friendly Relations and Co-operation among States" (hereinafter "resolution 2625 (XXV)"), in which it emphasized that "No territorial acquisition

[28] Vermeer and Akande (2019), pp. 50–54.

[29] UN Doc. A/RES/ESS-10/14.

[30] The 2004 ICJ Wall Advisory Opinion, para. 87.

> resulting from the threat or use of force shall be recognized as legal." As the Court stated in its Judgment in the case concerning Military and Paramilitary Activities in and against Nicaragua (Nicaragua v. United States of America), the principles as to the use of force incorporated in the Charter reflect customary international law (see I. C. J. Reports 1986, pp. 98–101, paras. 187–190); the same is true of its corollary entailing the illegality of territorial acquisition resulting from the threat or use of force.

On 30 December 2022, as mentioned earlier, the GA adopted another resolution A/RES/77/247 in which it requested the ICJ to give an additional advisory opinion on the following questions:[31]

> (a) What are the legal consequences arising from the ongoing violation by Israel of the right of the Palestinian people to self-determination, from its prolonged occupation, settlement and annexation of the Palestinian territory occupied since 1967, including measures aimed at altering the demographic composition, character and status of the Holy City of Jerusalem, and from its adoption of related discriminatory legislation and measures?
> (b) How do the policies and practices of Israel referred to ... above affect the legal status of the occupation, and what are the legal consequences that arise for all States and the United Nations from this status?

On 19 July 2024, the 2024 ICJ Advisory Opinion determined that Israel is violating PATBF.[32] On 18 September 2024, at the tenth ESS, the GA adopted a resolution regarding measures to be taken based on this Advisory Opinion.[33]

2.2.4 Continued Efforts Through Available Means

The dissatisfaction about existing territorial *status quo* should be weaker than in the inter-war period, but the unwillingness of States protected by the veto power to give up their power is still strong, and the limited acceptance of the ICJ's jurisdiction continues to limit the role of the judiciary in upholding rule of law against attempts to acquire territory by force. GA resolutions cannot substitute for Security Council resolutions adopted under Chapter VII, but when a GA resolution which clearly recognises the violation of rules relating to acquisition of territory by force is adopted with an overwhelming majority such as 140 in favour and less than 10 against, it has significant weight as the expression of States' considered legal opinions. Advisory Opinions of the ICJ are not legally binding, but when an Advisory Opinion clearly expresses its views that certain acts of a State violate rules relating to acquisition of territory by force, it also has significant authority, as the ICJ is the principal judicial organ of the UN.

After the Russian invasion of Ukraine in 2022 and Hamas's attack in 2023, there was criticism about a 'double standard' relating to the application of international law. To avoid double standards, a 'single' standard must be identified and upheld.

---

[31] UN Doc. A/RES/77/247.

[32] The 2024 ICJ Advisory Opinion, para. 179.

[33] UN Doc. A/ES-10/24.

As was indicated in the Security Council open debate held in January 2023, the majority of States seem to share a common interest in the maintenance of international peace and security based on the rule of law, and GA resolutions and the ICJ's Advisory Opinions should be utilised for the identification of a 'single' standard on the scope and effect of rules relating to attempts to acquire territory by force.

References

Akehurst, M. (1987). *A Modern Introduction to International Law*, 6th edn. Harper Collins

Brownlie, I. (1963). *International Law and the Use of Force by States*, Oxford University Press

Brunk, I. & Hakimi, M. (2024). The Prohibition of Annexations and the Foundations of Modern International Law, AJIL 118(3): 417–467

Carr, E.H. (1939). *The Twenty Years' Crisis, 1919–1939*. Palgrave Macmillan (reissued in 2016)

Clapham, A. (2012). *Brierly's Law of Nations*, 7th edn. Oxford University Press

De Wet, E. (2024). Article 42, in *The Charter of the United Nations A Commentary*, 4th edn. Vol. II, ed. By Simma B et al. Oxford University Press

Gray, C. (2018). *International Law and the Use of Force*, 4th edn. Oxford University Press

Greenwood, C. (1992). New World Order or Old? The Invasion of Kuwait and the Rule of Law, Modern Law Review 55

Jennings, R. & Watts, A. (ed.) (1992). *Oppenheim' International Law*, 9th edn. Volume I, Longman

Kennan, G. (1951). *American Diplomacy 1900–1950*, The University of Chicago Press (reissued in 2012)

Korman, S. (1996). The Right of conquest: The Acquisition of Territory by Force in International Law and Practice, Clarendon Press Oxford

Koskenniemi, M. (2001). Gentle Civilizer of Nations: The Rise and Fall of International Law 1870–1960. Cambridge University Press

Rostow, E.V. (1991). Until What? Enforcement Action or Collective Self-Defence, AJIL 85(3): 506–516

Shaw, M. (1991). International Law, 3rd edn. Grotius

Vermeer, Z. & Akande, D. (2019). Prior Consent by States to the Jurisdiction of International Courts and Tribunals in Inter-State Disputes. https://www.elac.ox.ac.uk/wp-content/uploads/2023/10/PriorConsent_Final_Report.pdf

Weston, B.H. (1991). Security Council Resolution 678 and Persian Gulf Decision Making, AJIL 85(3): 516–535

Wright, Q. (1932). The Stimson Note of January 7, 1932, AJIL 26(2): 342–348

Yanagihara, M. (2015). Significance of History of the Law of Nations in Europe and East Asia, Recueil des Cours 371: 277–435

Chapter 3
Scope of the Prohibition of Acquisition of Territory by Force (PATBF) and the Prohibition of Use of Force (PUF)

A State (hereinafter referred to as 'the deploying State') attempting to acquire territory by force typically deploys armed forces to an area of land which is not within its internationally recognised border nor under its existing administration, puts it under its control, expresses intention to exercise sovereignty and takes measures to annex it to its territory. This expression of intention to exercise sovereignty may take various forms, including declaration of such an intention, legislation to put the area of land in the territory and publication of an official map showing the area as its territory. The armed forces may be deployed without expressing intention to exercise sovereignty but putting the area effectively under its permanent control.

There might be other forms of attempts to acquire territory by force, but these forms seem to cover such cases as the Iraqi invasion of Kuwait in 1990 and Russia's invasion of Ukraine in 2022 and Israel's policies and practices in the OPT examined in the 2024 ICJ Advisory Opinion. Therefore, in the following examination of the scope and effect of PATBF and PUF, attempts to acquire territory by force are assumed to take these forms.[1]

As the acquisition of territory by force is prohibited under international law, from the legal point of view, States are not allowed to 'acquire' territory by force and their acts for acquiring territory do not amount to actual 'acquisition'. Therefore, legally speaking, their acts remain 'attempts' to acquire territory by force. The deploying State creates a situation where its newly established *de facto* control over the

[1] There might also be a possibility of acquisition of territory by 'threat' of force, but it is difficult to find a concrete example of attempts to acquire territory by threat of force alone. In this book, an attempt to acquire territory by force is assumed to take the form of the deployment of armed forces to an area of land which is beyond the deploying State's internationally recognised territory nor under its existing administration. In Sect. 3.4.5, whether such deployment of armed forces, even if it does not involve violent use of force, constitutes use of force under Article 2(4) of the UN Charter will be examined, without prejudice to the possibility of violating the prohibition of threat of force.

T. Mikanagi, *Toward Stronger Rule of Law Against Attempts to Acquire Territory by Force*, SpringerBriefs in Law,
https://doi.org/10.1007/978-981-95-2814-1_3

territory continues through the deterrent effect of the presence of armed forces against an actual or potential owner of territorial title over the territory. Through coercively creating *fait accompli* on the ground, the deploying State imposes new *status quo* on the ground and attempts to force the actual or potential owner of territorial title of the territory to accept its claim of sovereignty.

In the following, first, the relationship between PUF and PATBF will be examined in Sect. 3.1. After that, the method of analysis in this chapter and the next chapter will be explained in Sect. 3.2. Then, contextual elements contributing to the violation of PATBF and PUF will be examined in Sect. 3.3, and elements of acts involving use of force which contribute to the violation of PUF and PATBF will be examined in Sect. 3.4. In Sect. 3.5, hypothetical scenarios combining these elements will be examined as possible cases violating PUF and PATBF, and actions to be taken by States against attempts to acquire territory by force will be suggested. In a case where a State sends armed forces without revealing its involvement, the issue of attribution to the State would become an issue in applying PUF and PATBF. This issue will be addressed with reference to the situation in Crimea in 2014 in Sect. 3.6.

3.1 The Relationship Between PUF and PATBF

3.1.1 The ICJ's View on the Relationship Between the Two Prohibitions

The ICJ said in the 2004 Wall Advisory Opinion and in the 2024 Advisory Opinion that PATBF is a 'corollary' of PUF. The term 'corollary' used by the ICJ is ambiguous, but paragraph 253 of the 2024 Advisory Opinion reads as follows:[2]

> 253. The Court observes that an occupation involves, by its very nature, a continued use of force in foreign territory. Such use of force is, however, subject to the rules of international law governing the legality of the use of force or jus ad bellum. As indicated in Part V.C. above, these rules prohibit the use of force to acquire territory. Under contemporary international law as contained in the Charter of the United Nations and reflected in customary international law, occupation can under no circumstances serve as the source of title to territory or justify its acquisition by the occupying Power.

This paragraph seems to indicate that the ICJ considers PATBF to be a part of rules of international law governing the legality of the use of force or *jus ad bellum*.

Brunk and Hakimi argue that PUF and PATBF are different because the latter regulates territorial title, while Article 2(4) regulates the use of force. I agree with this distinction and the ICJ does not seem to deny this difference either. However,

[2] The 2024 ICJ Advisory Opinion, para. 253.

Brunk and Hakimi seem to argue for the stronger distinction between PUF and PATBF than the ICJ for three reasons.[3]

- The UN Charter recognizes two exceptions to Article 2(4), but PATBF applies even when the use of force is permissible.

This is an important question, and I will examine it as a matter of the effect of PATBF in Sect. 4.1 below. They also argue:

- The scope of application of Article 2(4) is itself open to debate, and PATBF should not be limited by debates about the scope of application of Article 2(4).

The ambiguity of the scope of Article 2(4) is problematic, but I will address this issue in Sect. 3.4 below. Brunk and Hakimi also point out:

- PATBF is distinct from PUF against territorial integrity or political independence and regulates title to territory. And that regulation of title to territory ties it to territorial entrenchment and self-determination.

With regard to the relationship between PATBF and the right of self-determination, the 1970 Declaration, while it is admittedly a result of political compromise, puts PATBF under the title of the 'principle that States shall refrain in their international relations from the threat or use of force against the territorial integrity or political independence of any State or in any other manner inconsistent with the purposes of the United Nations' rather than under the title of 'principle of equal rights and self-determination of peoples'. Furthermore, in the 2024 ICJ Advisory Opinion, the Court treated PATBF separately from the right of self-determination. In fact, in paragraph 179 of the Advisory Opinion, the Court found:[4]

> The Court has found that Israel's policies and practices amount to annexation of large parts of the Occupied Palestinian Territory. It is the view of the Court that to seek to acquire sovereignty over an occupied territory, as shown by the policies and practices adopted by Israel in East Jerusalem and the West Bank, is contrary to the prohibition of the use of force in international relations and its corollary principle of the non-acquisition of territory by force.

The ICJ put PUF and PATBF together and found their violation in one stroke. The right of self-determination is treated separately from PATBF and in determining the violation of PATBF the ICJ did not refer to the right of self-determination as an element constituting the violation. The Advisory Opinion applies PATBF in paragraphs 174–179 and deals with the question of self-determination in paragraphs 230–243. In other paragraphs, these two are treated as different norms.

As explained in the introduction, this book is written from the viewpoint of a practitioner who intends to use international law as a tool for upholding the rule of

---

[3] Brunk and Hakimi (2024), pp. 444–445.

[4] The 2024 ICJ Advisory Opinion, para. 179.

law against attempts to acquire territory by force. From this perspective, the opinion expressed by the ICJ in the 2024 Advisory Opinion and contents of the 1970 Friendly Relations Declaration should be respected. Therefore, in this book, I will treat PATBF and PUF as different prohibitions, but accept that PATBF is a corollary of PUF, respecting the ICJ's view and the categorisation in the 1970 Declaration. In addition, as the ICJ treated PATBF as a part of 'the rules of international law governing the legality of the use of force or *jus ad bellum*', an attempt to acquire territory by force which is prohibited by PATBF is assumed to involve use of force under Article 2(4) of the UN Charter.

3.1.2 Nature of PATBF and Two Types of PUF in the 1970 Declaration

To examine differences between PATBF and PUF, the basic nature of PATBF needs to be examined. Brunk and Hakimi argued that the regulation of territorial title must be the basic function of PATBF. As the prohibition of 'acquisition of territory' by force, it seems reasonable to assume that it has the function of denying the acquisition of territorial title through use of force. PUF does not necessarily have this function, and this function of PATBF seems likely to lead to the application of PATBF different from the application of PUF. With regard to PUF, the 1970 Declaration refers to the following two types of use of force:

Type I: Use of force 'to violate the existing international boundaries of another State' (hereinafter referred to as 'the Type I use of force').

Type II: Use of force 'as a means of settling international issues' and use of force 'as a means of solving international disputes, including territorial disputes and problems concerning frontiers of States' (hereinafter referred to as 'the Type II use of force').[5]

PATBF may apply to the deployment of armed forces which does not fall into the Type I use of force. In this sense, it has broader application than the prohibition of the Type I use of force. On the other hand, it does not necessarily apply to all the cases of the deployment of armed forces violating the prohibition of the Type II use of force. In this sense, it has narrower application than the prohibition of the Type II use of force. These two differences will be explained in the following.

[5] This type of use of force has some similarity with the type of war renounced in Article 1 of the Kellogg-Briand Pact quoted in Sect. 2.1.1 above.

3.1.3 PATBF and the Prohibition of the Type I Use of Force

PATBF may apply to the deployment of armed forces to an area of land which is not within another State's internationally recognised territory but has potential to become another State's territory. For example, in the 2024 Advisory Opinion, the ICJ applied PATBF to Israel's acts in the OPT, which was not yet regarded as another State's internationally recognised territory.[6] The OPT has the potential to become a territory of a new 'State of Palestine' in the future, but the 2024 Advisory Opinion did not recognise the existence of territorial sovereignty belonging to a 'State of Palestine'. What the ICJ did in this Advisory Opinion was to determine that Israel's acts designed to exercise permanent control over the OPT, which has the potential to become the territory of a new 'State of Palestine' through a peace process but was not yet treated by the ICJ as the territory of the 'State of Palestine', violate PATBF. Therefore, the 2024 Advisory Opinion indicates that PATBF prohibit not only acts involving use of force in another State's internationally recognised territory, which would fall into the Type I use of force above, but also acts involving use of force in territory which has potential to become another State's territory. In this sense, PATBF has broader application than the prohibition of the Type I use of force.

3.1.4 PATBF and the Prohibition of the Type II Use of Force

'Territory which has potential to become another State's territory' may also refer to an area of land which is claimed by another State and of which the latter State has been consolidating territorial title. Whether PATBF applies to an area of land which does not belong to another State's internationally recognised territory but is subject to competing claims by States[7] will be examined in detail in Sects. 3.3.3.4 and 3.3.3.5. However, to explain the difference in the application of PUF and PATBF, preliminary examination of PATBF's application to territory subject to competing claims seems necessary at this stage.

If there are no other claimants making competing claims over an area of land, a State attempting to exercise control over the area does not have to use armed forces for deterring or countering challenges from other claimants. On the other hand, if the area in question is claimed by another State (State A), a State (State B) which is attempting to acquire control over the area may need to use armed forces for

[6] In para. 283 of the 2024 Advisory Opinion, the ICJ considered that 'the realization of the right of the Palestinian people to self-determination, including its right to an independent and sovereign State, living side by side in peace with the State of Israel within secure and recognized borders for both States, as envisaged in resolutions of the Security Council and General Assembly, would contribute to regional stability and the security of all States in the Middle East.' This paragraph implies that Palestinian people have not yet realised the right to an independent and sovereign State.

[7] The intention behind the use of the term 'an area of land, or territory, subject to competing claims' is explained in Sect. 3.3.1 below.

deterring or countering challenges from State A. In this case, typically, State B would deploy armed forces to the area, put it under its control, create *fait accompli* through the presence of armed forces and force State A to accept State B's claim. This State B's deployment of armed forces is likely to amount to the Type II use of force mentioned above.[8]

However, if State B has a stronger territorial title than State A,[9] does PATBF apply to State B's deployment of armed forces? If it is accepted that PATBF has the function of denying the acquisition of 'territorial title' rather than 'control over territory' by force, when State B has stronger territorial title than State A, as the purpose of State B's deployment of armed forces is, in fact, the acquisition of control over the territory rather than the acquisition of territorial title, it would not violate PATBF in its strict sense. If this strict understanding is correct, PATBF has a narrower scope of application than the prohibition of Type II use of force.[10] If the function of denying the acquisition of territorial title through use of force adds particular significance to PATBF and this particular significance gives additional gravity to the violation of PATBF, the strict understanding above seems appropriate. Furthermore, the obligation for third States not to recognise the acquisition of territory by force is difficult to apply in a case where State B has stronger territorial title than State A. While the question above deserves further discussion, in this book, this strict understanding of PATBF is adopted and it is assumed that, if State B has a stronger territorial title than State A, State B is not attempting to acquire territorial title and, therefore, the prohibition of 'acquisition of territory' by force does not apply to the deployment of armed forces by State B.

3.1.5 Can the ICJ Apply PATBF to Territory Subject to Competing Claims?

On the other hand, this strict understanding of PATBF makes its application rather difficult in cases where State A and State B have competing claims and their relative strength of territorial title is not known. If PATBF does not apply to cases where the deploying State has stronger territorial title, to apply PATBF to an area of land subject to competing claims, State A must have territorial title at least as strong as State B. When there is no available decision by a third-party dispute settlement body like the ICJ on the strength of territorial title, it would be difficult for third States to

[8] The application of the prohibition of the Type II use of force will be examined in Sect. 3.3.1 below.

[9] As an example, as will be examined in Sect. 3.3.3.2 below, Eritrea, which had a strong territorial title over Badme, deployed armed forces to Badme in 1998, and in 2005 it was found to have violated PUF by the Eritrea-Ethiopia Claims Commission.

[10] Klein and Koutroulis also distinguish between the principle that 'acquisition or transfer of sovereignty over a territory as a result of the threat or use of force is illegal' and the principle that 'threat or use of force in order to resolve a territorial dispute is prohibited'. See Klein and Koutroulis (2018), p. 235–261.

know the relative strength of State A and State B's territorial title. Furthermore, even if a case relating to the deployment of armed forces is brought before a third-party dispute settlement body, State B might try to rely on the ambiguity about the relative strength of territorial title at the time of the deployment. In such a case, to what extent would State B be allowed to rely on this 'ambiguity' about the relative strength of territorial title? Can a third-party dispute settlement body like the ICJ overcome this plea of 'ambiguity' and apply PATBF to State B's deployment of armed forces to territory subject to competing claims? If State B can rely on this 'ambiguity' to avoid the application of PATBF as long as it insists on the existence of 'ambiguity', PATBF would become impossible to apply to a case where State B makes territorial claim competing with State A. While it is difficult to say to what extent State B can rely on the plea of 'ambiguity', to avoid a self-judging type of loophole in the application of PATBF, there must be a limit.

More detailed analysis about cases where PATBF applies to territory subject to competing claims will be made in Sects. 3.3.3.4 and 3.3.3.5, but, as the above question naturally arises from the examination of the relationship between PATBF and PUF, a possible case where PATBF may apply to territory subject to competing claims should be indicated at this stage. In the following case, a third-party dispute settlement body like the ICJ, when referred to, may find not only State A's sovereignty over the territory but also State B's violation of PATBF.

- State A has been openly and constantly taking administrative measures regulating activities in an area of land long enough to consolidate territorial title. State B has become aware of State A's administrative measures regulating activities in the area but has not protested.[11]
- There is no treaty between State A and State B referring to the area as State B's territory, and State B has not been taking administrative measures regulating activities in the area.
- After years of failure to respond to State A's peaceful administrative measures, State B starts to protest and deploys armed forces to the territory. After occupying the territory, State B declares its annexation.
- Initially, State B refuses to go to the ICJ. However, after years of calls from third States and a change in State B's government, State B agrees to bring the case before the ICJ.
- The ICJ finds State A's sovereignty over the territory based on the consolidation of territorial title through peaceful administrative measures.

Can the ICJ also apply PATBF to State B's acts? In this case, State B's awareness of State A's administrative measures and its failure to protest, coupled with the absence of treaty or administrative measures supporting State B's territorial title, should make it difficult for State B to argue that it honestly believed that it had stronger territorial title based on international law than State A. If the ICJ cannot apply PATBF even in this kind of case, it would become difficult to imagine a case where

[11] See Case 1.1 in Sect. 3.3.3.4 below.

PATBF is applicable to the deployment of armed forces to territory subject to competing claims, and PATBF might become applicable only to cases involving internationally recognised territory or situations like the OPT, where there have been Security Council or GA resolutions supporting the application of PATBF.[12] In view of the effectiveness of PATBF, in the following, it is assumed that third-party dispute settlement bodies like the ICJ may apply PATBF to cases like the example above and PATBF may apply to the deployment of armed forces to territory subject to competing claims in some cases.

In cases like the example above where third-party dispute settlement bodies like the ICJ may apply PATBF to the deployment of armed forces to territory subject to competing claims, while such findings are not yet available, the prohibition of the Type II use of force may be easier to apply for third States, as will be examined in Sect. 3.3.3.2 below. In this sense, in cases relating to territory subject to competing claims, the prohibition of the Type II use of force may work as an alternative rule of international law against potential attempts to acquire territory by force.

3.1.6 Difference in the Timing of the Application of PUF and PATBF

In addition to the difference in the scope of application, another possible difference between PUF and PATBF may lie in their timing of application. If the deploying State does not declare its annexation and does not take measures to formally annex it, it would not be clear if the occupation itself amounts to the acquisition of territory by force. In the case of the Russian invasion of Ukraine in 2022, the invasion started in February 2022, and it immediately violated the prohibition of Type I use of force above; and the measures to annex four regions of Ukraine were taken in September and October 2022 and they violated PATBF. Similar sequence of the violations of PUF and PATBF may also take place in the case of the deployment of armed forces to territory subject to competing claims, if the deploying State violates the prohibition of Type II use of force through occupation of the territory first and then violates PATBF by starting to annex the occupied territory. However, in addition, the deploying State may have already taken some measures to annex the territory in question before the deployment of armed forces, without taking effect on the ground, and these measures take effect on the ground immediately after it establishes control over the territory. Therefore, in such cases, the deployment and occupation may violate both PUF and PATBF at the same time.

[12] See Sect. 3.3.2 below.

3.2 Methods of Analysis in Chaps. 3 and 4

3.2.1 Interpretation of Article 2(4) and Identification of Customary Law

In the judgment on Case Concerning Military and Paramilitary Activities in and against Nicaragua (Nicaragua v. United States of America) in 1986 (the Nicaragua ICJ Judgment), the ICJ examined if PUF under Article 2(4) of the UN Charter became customary international law, and said: 'The Court must satisfy itself that the existence of the rule in the *opinio juris* of States is confirmed by practice.'[13] The Court further continued as follows:[14]

> …This *opinio juris* may, though with all due caution, be deduced from, *inter alia*, the attitude of States towards certain General Assembly resolutions, and particularly resolution 2625 (XXV) entitled "Declaration on Principles of International Law concerning Friendly Relations and Co-operation among States in accordance with the Charter of the United Nations". The effect of consent to the text of such resolutions cannot be understood as merely that of a "reiteration or elucidation" of treaty commitment undertaken in the Charter. On the contrary, it may be understood as an acceptance of the validity of the rule or set of rules declared by the resolution by themselves. The principle of non-use of force, for example may thus be regarded as a principle of customary international law, …

This paragraph of the Nicaragua judgment indicates that the ICJ considers the contents of the 1970 Declarations relating to the principle of non-use of force to be both 'reiteration or elucidation' of treaty commitment undertaken in the UN Charter and an acceptance of the validity of the rule or set of rules declared by the resolution as customary international law. On this unique dual character of the Friendly Relations Declaration as evidence for both the interpretation of Article 2(4) and the identification of corresponding customary international law, Olivier Corten wrote: 'The text of the Declaration is therefore remarkably interesting in terms both of the establishment of a customary legal rule but also of the interpretation of a treaty, to wit the UN Charter'. He also wrote: 'It is incontrovertible that the Friendly Relations Declaration is indeed a "subsequent agreement between the parties" that can be used to determine the meaning of the relevant provisions of the Charter concerning *jus contra bellum'*.[15]

Therefore, PUF has dual nature of prohibition under Article 2(4) and a customary rule of international law, and the 1970 Declaration provides evidence for both aspects. As mentioned above, PATBF is assumed to involve use of force under Article 2(4) of the UN Charter, and it also needs to be examined through the dual approach based both on the interpretation of Article 2(4) of the UN Charter and on

[13] Case Concerning Military and Paramilitary Activities in and against Nicaragua (Nicaragua v. United States of America), Judgment, 27 June 1986, ICJ Rep. (1986) [hereinafter cited as the Nicaragua judgment], para. 184.

[14] Ibid. Para. 188.

[15] Corten (2020), p. 52.

the identification of a rule of customary international law, and the 1970 Declaration provides evidence for both aspects of PATBF.

3.2.2 Evidence for Treaty Interpretation and Customary Rule

3.2.2.1 GA Resolutions Other than the 1970 Declaration

The interpretation of Article 2(4) of the UN Charter must be based on the basic rules of interpretation clarified in Articles 31 and 32 of the Vienna Convention on the Law of Treaties (VCLT), which provide:[16]

> **Article 31** General rule of interpretation
> 1. A treaty shall be interpreted in good faith in accordance with the ordinary meaning to be given to the terms of the treaty in their context and in the light of its object and purpose. ...
> 3. There shall be taken into account, together with the context:
> (a) any subsequent agreement between the parties regarding the interpretation of the treaty or the application of its provisions;
> (b) any subsequent practice in the application of the treaty which establishes the agreement of the parties regarding its interpretation; ...
> **Article 32** Supplementary means of interpretation
> Recourse may be had to supplementary means of interpretation, including the preparatory work of the treaty and the circumstances of its conclusion, in order to confirm the meaning resulting from the application of article 31, or to determine the meaning when the interpretation according to article 31:
> (a) leaves the meaning ambiguous or obscure; or
> (b) leads to a result which is manifestly absurd or unreasonable.

The International Law Commission (ILC) studied the subsequent agreement and practice mentioned in Article 31(3)(a) and (b) and adopted 'The Conclusions on Subsequent Agreements and Subsequent Practice in Relation to the Interpretation of Treaties'. The conclusions and articles with commentaries which have been adopted by the ILC after careful discussions among its members have significant weight as authority in understanding international law. The reports of the ILC often provide important information for the ICJ judges. Furthermore, members of the ILC are often elected to be the ICJ judges. Therefore, in the following, relevant works of the ILC will be referred to as an important reference.

The ILC's commentary on the 'Conclusions on Subsequent Agreements and Subsequent Practice in Relation to the Interpretation of Treaties' refers to the GA resolutions as follows:[17]

> (20) The International Court of Justice, although it did not expressly mention article 31, paragraph 3 (a), when relying on the General Assembly Declaration on Friendly Relations between States for the interpretation of Article 2, paragraph 4, of the Charter, emphasized

---

[16] United Nations, Treaty Series, vol. 1155, p. 331. https://legal.un.org/ilc/texts/instruments/english/conventions/1_1_1969.pdf

[17] UN Doc. A/73/10, p. 99.

> the "attitude of the Parties and the attitude of States towards certain General Assembly resolutions" and their consent thereto. In this context, a number of writers have concluded that subsequent agreements within the meaning of article 31, paragraph 3 (a), may, under certain circumstances, arise from or be expressed in acts of plenary organs of international organizations, such as the General Assembly of the United Nations. Indeed, as the WTO Appellate Body has Indicated with reference to the Commission, the characterization of a collective decision as an "authentic element of interpretation" under article 31, paragraph 3 (a), is only justified if the parties of the constituent instrument of an international organization acted as such and not, as they usually do, institutionally as members of the respective plenary organ.

Conclusions 5 and 9 of the ILC's 'Conclusions on Subsequent Agreements and Subsequent Practice in Relation to the Interpretation of Treaties' explain what constitutes subsequent practice and which subsequent agreements and practice have weight as a means of interpretation. They read:[18]

> **Conclusion 5** Conduct as subsequent practice
>
> 1. Subsequent practice under articles 31 and 32 may consist of any conduct of a party in the application of a treaty, whether in the exercise of its executive, legislative, judicial, or other functions.
>
> **Conclusion 9** Weight of subsequent agreements and subsequent practice as a means of interpretation
>
> 1. The weight of a subsequent agreement or subsequent practice as a means of interpretation under article 31, paragraph 3, depends, inter alia, on its clarity and specificity.
> 2. In addition, the weight of subsequent practice under article 31, paragraph 3 (b), depends, inter alia, on whether and how it is repeated.
> 3. The weight of subsequent practice as a supplementary means of interpretation under article 32 may depend on the criteria referred to in paragraphs 1 and 2.

GA resolutions other than the 1970 Declarations may, if they represent conduct of Member States of the United Nations in the application of the UN Charter, also be taken into account as subsequent practice or agreement under Article 31(3)(a) and (b) of the VCLT. Their weight as a means of interpretation depends, inter alia, on their clarity and specificity. Conclusion 4 also reads:[19]

> **Conclusion 4** Definition of subsequent agreement and subsequent practice
>
> 3. A subsequent practice as a supplementary means of interpretation under article 32 consists of conduct by one or more parties in the application of the treaty, after its conclusion.

Even if GA resolutions are not adopted by consensus, they may be referred to as a supplementary means under Article 32 of the VCLT, and their weight also depends on clarity and specificity. Their weight would also be affected by the number of Member States supporting them.

Regarding the identification of the content of PATBF as a rule of customary international law, in the Nicaragua judgment, the ICJ treated PUF as a rule of customary international law and pointed out the significance of general conduct of States in identifying a rule of customary international law. The ICJ said:[20]

---

[18] Ibid. p. 14.

[19] Ibid. p. 13.

[20] The Nicaragua judgment, para. 186.

> 186. … The Court does not consider that, for a rule to be established as customary, the corresponding practice must be in absolutely rigorous conformity with the rule. In order to deduce the existence of customary rules, the Court deems it sufficient that the conduct of States should, in general, be consistent with such rules, and that instances of State conduct inconsistent with a given rule should generally have been treated as breaches of that rule, not as indications of the recognition of a new rule. If a State acts in a way prima facie incompatible with a recognized rule, but defends its conduct by appealing to exceptions or justifications contained within the rule itself, then whether or not the State's conduct is in fact justifiable on that basis, the significance of that attitude is to confirm rather than to weaken the rule.

In examining the scope and effect of PATBF as a rule of customary international law, this general conduct of States should be taken into account. GA resolutions are not legally binding, but when a State supports a GA resolution showing a clear position on the content of PATBF, it can be regarded as expression of the State's position on PATBF. The ILC also adopted the 'Draft conclusions on identification of customary international law'. Conclusion 12 of the draft conclusions provides:[21]

> **Conclusion 12** Resolutions of international organizations and intergovernmental conferences
>
> …
>
> 2. A resolution adopted by an international organization or at an intergovernmental conference may provide evidence for determining the existence and content of a rule of customary international law, or contribute to its development.
>
> 3. A provision in a resolution adopted by an international organization or at an intergovernmental conference may reflect a rule of customary international law if it is established that the provision corresponds to a general practice that is accepted as law (*opinio juris*).

Therefore, GA resolutions 'may' provide evidence for determining the scope and effect of rules relating to acquisition of territory by force as rules of customary international law. The commentary on paragraph 2 of this conclusion reads:[22]

> The word "may" seeks to caution that not all resolutions serve such a role. As the International Court of Justice has observed, resolutions "even if they are not binding … can, in certain circumstances, provide evidence important for establishing the existence of a rule or the emergence of an *opinio juris*". This is particularly so when a resolution purports to be declaratory of an existing rule of customary international law, in which case it may serve as evidence of the acceptance as law of such a rule by those States supporting the resolution. In other words, "[t]he effect of consent to the text of such resolutions … may be understood as an acceptance of the validity of the rule or set of rules declared by the resolution". Conversely, negative votes, abstentions or disassociations from a consensus, along with general statements and explanations of positions, may be evidence that there is no acceptance as law.

Therefore, some GA resolutions other than the 1970 Declarations may provide evidence for determining the existence and content of rules of customary international law, if they purport to be declaratory of existing rules of customary international law.

In fact, as will be mentioned in the following, in the 2024 Advisory Opinion, the ICJ referred to various GA resolutions other than the 1970 Declarations in applying

[21] Ibid. p. 121.

[22] Ibid. p. 148.

PATBF. These references strongly indicate the Court's reliance on these GA resolutions as evidence for the interpretation of the UN Charter and the identification of customary international law.

3.2.2.2 Views of International Courts and Tribunals

The ICJ's decisions and opinions should be given a particular weight in the interpretation of the UN Charter, considering the ICJ's status as the principal judicial organ of the United Nations. In addition, and as already mentioned, the ICJ's judgments and opinions have practical significance for practitioners of international law who intend to use the ICJ as tool for upholding the rule of law against acquisition of territory by force.

In the context of the identification of customary international law, Conclusion 13 of the 'Draft conclusions on identification of customary international law' reads:[23]

> **Conclusion 13** Decisions of courts and tribunals
> 1. Decisions of international courts and tribunals, in particular of the International Court of Justice, concerning the existence and content of rules of customary international law are a subsidiary means for the determination of such rules.

This includes not only the ICJ but also other international courts and tribunals.

3.2.2.3 Academic Literature

Article 38(1)(d) of the ICJ State provides that the ICJ shall apply the 'teachings of the most highly qualified publicists of the various nations', as subsidiary means for the determination of rules of law.

Conclusion 14 of the 'Draft conclusions on identification of customary international law' also refers to the teachings, which reads:[24]

> **Conclusion 14** Teachings
> Teachings of the most highly qualified publicists of the various nations may serve as a subsidiary means for the determination of rules of customary international law.

In the following, in examining the current state of rules relating to acquisition of territory by force, academic literature which appears to be influential in the discussion of relevant issues will be referred to.

[23] Ibid. p. 121.
[24] Ibid. p. 121.

3.2.3 Analytical Framework in Chap. 3

As mentioned above, acts violating PATBF, which is a corollary of PUF, are assumed to involve use of force under Article 2(4). The application of PUF and the application of PATBF require not only the examination of acts involving use of force but also the examination of their contexts.

Erin Pobjie writes in her book: 'a 'use of force' is a 'type', characterised by a basket of elements which do not all have to be present and which must be weighed and balanced to determine whether the threshold for the definition is met and an act is an unlawful 'use of force' under article 2(4) of the UN Charter'.[25] In her 'type theory', Pobjie advocates combined analysis of multiple elements in applying Article 2(4) of the UN Charter. As elements to be weighed and balanced, she refers to 'contextual elements' and elements of 'use of force.'[26] The Japanese government also takes a similar approach in applying rules relating to use of force. A typical answer by Japanese government officials to a Diet (Parliament) question on the determination of the existence of an armed attack is:[27]

> As for the question on how to determine the point of the initiation of an armed attack, specific means and modality of an armed attack may vary. It may take such forms as bombardment, missile attack, and cross-border invasions by armed forces. Therefore, it would be necessary to take into account overall circumstances including the international situation, intention, means and modality to determine the specific point of the initiation of an armed attack.

The second sentence quoted above and Erin Pobjie's 'type theory' seem to have similarities. 'The international situation' in this Diet answer corresponds to Erin Pobjie's 'contextual elements', and 'intention, means and modality' correspond to her elements of 'use of force'. These elements constitute 'overall circumstances' to be taken into account, which correspond to her 'basket of elements'. While this Diet answer concerns an armed attack and Erin Pobjie's 'type theory' concerns use of force, according to the ICJ's Nicaragua judgment,[28] an armed attack is 'the most grave forms of the use of force', and the approach taken in determining the existence of an armed attack naturally has similarity with the approach taken in determining what constitutes use of force prohibited under Article 2(4) of the UN Charter.

As attempts to acquire territory by force may take various forms in various contexts, the analytical framework for the application of relevant prohibitions should have sufficient flexibility. In the following, various elements contributing to the violation of the two prohibitions will be identified first, and possible scenarios based on the combination of these elements will be examined in the search for possible thresholds for their violation. The relevant elements can be categorised into 'acts',

---

[25] Pobjie (2024), p. 229.

[26] Ibid. pp. 229–230.

[27] Mikanagi and Ogi (2016), p. 363.

[28] The Nicaragua judgment, para. 191.

which constitute use of force and the acquisition of territory by force, and their 'contexts'.

As candidates for such elements contributing to the violation of PATBF and PUF, the following will be examined:

Contextual elements
- Internationally recognised territory of another State
- Peaceful administration by another State
- Peacefully established administration by another State
- Longstanding peacefully established administration by another State
- Resort to use of force as a means of settlement despite available third-party dispute settlement mechanism

Elements of acts involving use of force
- Use of armed force
- Coercive intention
- Gravity of use of force
- Establishment of control through coercive measures
- Explicit measures to annex territory
- Conduct establishing permanent control

Some of these elements might constitute pre-conditions required for the application of PUF and PATBF. Which elements constitute such pre-conditions will also be examined in the following. These elements should hopefully also serve as a 'check list' for the application of PUF and PATBF. After examining these elements, hypothetical scenarios combining these elements will be examined as possible cases violating PUF and PATBF. In addition, actions to be taken by third States and UN organs against attempts to acquire territory by force in these scenarios will also be suggested.

3.3 Contextual Elements

3.3.1 PUF's Applicability to Territory Subject to Competing Claims

The expression of 'territory subject to competing claims' is used here instead of 'disputed territory', because in some cases, especially where a State has been peacefully administering territory without facing protest from other States for many years, the existence of dispute itself becomes a serious contentious issue. While the term 'disputed' may sound as if there has been a longstanding dispute, the term 'subject to competing claims' here is intended to refer to the current situation only without indicating the continuous existence of a dispute. For the third States, whether there are, currently, competing claims over territory or not can be determined based on objective facts, and the term 'territory subject to competing claims' used in this sense should be, hopefully, comparatively less likely to offend a State denying the existence of dispute than the term 'disputed territory'. Therefore, in the following, the term 'territory subject to competing claims' will be preferred to the term 'disputed territory'.

As mentioned in Sect. 3.1.2 above, the paragraphs of the 1970 Declaration relating to PUF refer to the following two types of uses of force:[29]

The Type I use of force: Use of force 'to violate the existing international boundaries of another State'.

The Type II use of force: Use of force 'as a means of settling international issues' and use of force 'as a means of solving international disputes, including territorial disputes and problems concerning frontiers of States'.

When an area of land is subject to competing territorial claims of States, from third States' point of view, there is an international issue or a territorial dispute among the States concerned relating to the sovereignty of the territory. Therefore, when one of the States, which has not been administering the area, deploys armed forces to the territory to put it under its control, it is likely to amount to the Type II use of force. Therefore, the 1970 Declaration strongly indicates that PUF applies to the deployment of armed forces by one of the claimants to an area of land which has been claimed by two or more States, including the deploying State, and has not been under the deploying State's administration.[30]

The 2005 Partial Award of the Eritrea–Ethiopia Claims Commission (EECC) examined whether Eritrea violated Article 2(4) of the UN Charter by attacking and occupying in 1998 the town of Badme, whose sovereignty was claimed by Eritrea but which the Commission found was under 'peaceful administration' by Ethiopia at the time. The Commission recognised that the existence of territorial disputes does not preclude the applicability of the prohibition of the threat or use of force. It noted:[31]

> ... border disputes between States are so frequent that any exception to the prohibition of the threat or use of force for territory that is allegedly occupied unlawfully would create a large and dangerous hole in a fundamental rule of international law.

On 16 December 2015, the ICJ delivered a judgment on the case concerning Certain Activities Carried out by Nicaragua in the Border Area (Costa Rica v Nicaragua), which was combined with the case concerning Construction of a Road in Costa Rica along the San Juan River (Nicaragua v Costa Rica). In this judgment, the ICJ found: 'Costa Rica has sovereignty over the "disputed territory" as defined by the Court.'[32]

---

[29] UN Doc. A/RES/2625(XXV).

[30] Mikanagi (2018), pp. 1022–1024. For a more comprehensive compilation of relevant cases, see Yiallourides, Gehring and Gauci (2018).

[31] Eritrea–Ethiopia Claims Commission, Partial Award, Jus ad Bellum: Ethiopia's Claims 1–8, 19 December 2005, RIAA 26 [hereinafter cited as the 2005 EECC Partial Award], p. 465, para 10.

[32] Certain Activities Carried out by Nicaragua in the Border Area (Costa Rica v Nicaragua) and Construction of a Road in Costa Rica along the San Juan River (Nicaragua v Costa Rica), Merits,

The Court also found: 'by excavating three caños [channels] and establishing a military presence on Costa Rican territory, Nicaragua has violated the territorial sovereignty of Costa Rica'. Costa Rica asked the ICJ to find that by occupying and claiming the Costa Rican territory Nicaragua breached the prohibition of the threat or use of force under Article 2(4) of the UN Charter. On this matter, the ICJ said:[33]

> … in the circumstances, given that the unlawful character of these activities has already been established, the Court need not dwell any further on this submission. As in the case concerning Land and Maritime Boundary between Cameroon and Nigeria (Cameroon v. Nigeria Equatorial Guinea intervening), the Court finds that 'by the very fact of the present Judgment and of the evacuation' of the disputed territory, the injury suffered by Costa Rica 'will in all events have been sufficiently addressed'.

However, in this judgment the ICJ also said:

> The fact that Nicaragua considered that its activities were taking place on its own territory does not exclude the possibility of characterizing them as an unlawful use of force.

Thus, the Court did not deny the applicability of PUF to the deployment of armed forces to the area of land subject to competing claims by States.

Academic literature also seems to support the applicability. On the application of PUF to territory subject to competing claims by States, Olivier Corten refers to the paragraphs of the 1970 Declaration relating to the Type II use of force and argues that Article 2(4) of the UN Charter needs to be interpreted in conjunction with Article 2(3) which prescribes the peaceful settlement of dispute and that PUF is applicable beyond a cross-border armed action. He concludes that, when a territory is under the *de facto* control of State B, even if it actually belongs to State A, should State A intervene militarily in the territory, the rule prohibiting the use of force applies.[34]

Christian Tams examined this issue in his commentary on Article 2(4).[35] He also quotes the part of the 1970 Declarations relating to the Type II use of force, and the same parts of the ICJ judgment on the Costa Rica v Nicaragua case as Corten and the award by the Eritrea-Ethiopia Claims Commission as quoted above. He concluded:

> These statements are informed by a keen (and understandable) desire to avoid loopholes in the ban on force. Yet, as has been observed avoiding loopholes comes at a price: to the extent that the validity of title is considered irrelevant, Article 2(4) prima facie applies to the recovery of occupied lands even where these lands have been occupied in blatant violation of international law. As far as interpretation of the terms 'in their international relations' is concerned, this reading has been endorsed in international practice, but it means that arguments for forcible recovery need to be articulated on the basis of exceptions to Art 2(4), notably self-defence.

Judgment, 16 December 2015, ICJ Rep. (2015) [hereinafter cited as the Costa Rica v Nicaragua judgment], p. 740, para. 229.

[33] Ibid. para. 97.

[34] Corten (2010), p. 149.

[35] Tams (2024), pp. 332–333.

Both Corten and Tams seem to support the applicability of PUF to the deployment of armed forces to territory subject to competing claims by States.

Based on the foregoing, it seems reasonable to confirm that PUF is applicable to the deployment of armed forces by one of the claimants to territory which is subject to claims by multiple States. Whether PATBF is also applicable to such territory has been preliminarily examined in Sect. 3.1.2 above and will be examined in more detail in Sects. 3.3.3.4 and 3.3.3.5.

3.3.2 Applicability to Acts Not Taking Place Between States

Olivier Corten devotes one chapter of his book 'The Law Against War' to the question: 'Do the prohibition of the use of force and self-defence apply to non-state actors?'[36] In this chapter, he explains why PUF does not apply to national liberation struggles, arguing that there is no agreement among States on its applicability to national liberation struggles.

In addition to the references to the Type I use of force and the Type II use of force mentioned above, the 1970 Declaration also has a sentence stating that '[e]very State likewise has the duty to refrain from the threat or use of force to violate international lines of demarcation, such as armistice lines, established by or pursuant to an international agreement to which it is a party or which it is otherwise bound to respect'. This sentence does not appear to exclude a situation where an international line of demarcation exists between a State and a non-State actor. However, according to Corten, '[t]he *travaux preparatoires* shows that, what was finally in view were the lines separating the territories of two States and not a territorial boundary of any non-State entity.'[37]

As discussed above, in paragraph 87 of the 2004 Wall Advisory Opinion, the ICJ said that PATBF is a corollary of PUF, and, in paragraph 121, the Court said:[38]

> 121. Whilst the Court notes the assurance given by Israel that the construction of the wall does not amount to annexation and that the wall is of a temporary nature (see paragraph 116 above), it nevertheless cannot remain indifferent to, certain fears expressed to it that the route of the wall will prejudge the future frontier between Israel and Palestine, and the fear that Israel may integrate the settlements and their means of access. The Court considers that the construction of the wall and its associated régime create a "fait accompli" on the ground that could well become permanent, in which case, and notwithstanding the formal characterization of the wall by Israel, it would be tantamount to de facto annexation.

Corten concedes that this Advisory Opinion 'might suggest that the prohibition of the use of force is a rule applicable between a State (here Israel) and a people with the right to self-determination (the Palestinian people)', but he nevertheless concludes that '[s]uch a conclusion would be excessive, for two reasons.' These two

[36] Corten (2010), p. 126.

[37] Corten (2020), p. 58; Corten (2010), pp. 138–146.

[38] The ICJ Wall Advisory Opinion, para. 121.

reasons are the ICJ's reference to 'green line' as the armistice line agreed with Jordan in 1948 and the Court's denial of the application of the right to self-defence under Article 51 of the UN Charter.[39]

On the other hand, Christian Tams considers the reference to 'international lines of demarcation' in the 1970 Declaration to be the strongest textual support for treating force against *de facto* regimes as part of a State's 'international relations' mentioned in Article 2(4) of the UN Charter.[40] He argues:

> …the most convincing approach is to consider that de facto regimes are covered by Art 2(4)'s reference to 'international relations' only if they have been stabilized over a sustained period of time and if they (while not qualifying as a State under the declaratory theory) can be 'assimilated to a State, because of [their] sustained effective government of a given territory'.[41]

They seem to have different opinions on the application of Article 2(4) to acts taking place not between States.

Regarding the Occupied Palestinian Territory (OPT), preambular paragraph 2 of Security Council resolution 242 adopted on 22 November 1967 emphasises 'the inadmissibility of the acquisition of territory by war'. It also affirmed that the fulfilment of Charter principles requires the establishment of a just and lasting peace in the Middle East which should include the application of principles including the '[w]ithdrawal of Israel armed forces from territories occupied in the recent conflict'.

Article 2(4) of the UN Charter refers to 'the Purposes of the United Nations', and Article 1(1) of the UN Charter, which stipulates the purpose of the United Nations, should constitute an important context and object and purpose for the interpretation of Article 2(4). The Security Council has the primary responsibility for the maintenance of international peace and security, and its view on the purpose of the United Nations might have a certain weight in determining whether PUF and PATBF apply to certain territory. On the other hand, Corten takes the position that the Security Council's role is much more limited than the General Assembly in elaborating customary international law.[42]

As a relevant GA Resolution, the GA adopted resolution 77/126 on 15 December 2022, 18 days before requesting ICJ's second advisory opinion. This resolution refers to PATBF in the preamble, and in OP7, after recalling PATBF, it refers to the illegality of the annexation of the OPT. The relevant parts of the resolution read:[43]

> The General Assembly,
>
> Guided by the principles and purposes of the Charter of the United Nations and the need to respect the obligations arising from the Charter and other instruments and rules of international law,
>
> Reaffirming the inadmissibility of the acquisition of territory by force, …

[39] Corten (2010), p. 147.

[40] Tams (2024), p. 334.

[41] Ibid. p. 335.

[42] Corten (2010), p. 45.

[43] UN Doc. A/RES/77/126.

> 7. Stresses that the occupation of a territory is to be a temporary, de facto situation, whereby the occupying Power can neither claim possession nor exert its sovereignty over the territory it occupies, recalls in this regard the principle of the inadmissibility of the acquisition of land by force and therefore the illegality of the annexation of any part of the Occupied Palestinian Territory, including East Jerusalem, which constitutes a breach of international law, undermines the viability of the two-State solution and challenges the prospects for a just, lasting and comprehensive peace settlement, and expresses its grave concern at recent statements calling for the annexation by Israel of areas in the Occupied Palestinian Territory; ...

This resolution was adopted by 141 votes to 7, with 21 abstentions.[44] This resolution indicates that 141 Member States supporting this resolution considered that PATBF applies to the OPT.

The 2024 ICJ Advisory Opinion did not clearly explain why PATBF applies to Israel's acts in the OPT, but after referring to PATBF as a corollary of PUF, the Court took note of relevant Security Council resolutions, including resolution 242, in paragraph 176:[45]

> 176. In this regard, the Court observes that the prohibition of acquisition of territory by force was emphasized by the Security Council in its resolution 242 (1967) of 22 November 1967 (see paragraph 58 above). The Security Council affirmed this principle by resolution 252 (1968) of 21 May 1968, where it also declared that "all legislative and administrative measures and actions taken by Israel, including expropriation of land and properties thereon, which tend to change the legal status of Jerusalem are invalid and cannot change that status". The Security Council has since reiterated this principle in several resolutions dealing with Israel's purported annexation of Arab and Palestinian territory (for example, Security Council resolutions 267 (1969) of 1 April 1969, 298 (1971) of 25 September 1971 and 478 (1980) of 20 August 1980). More recently, the Security Council, in its resolution 2334 (2016) of 23 December 2016, stated that
>
> > "the establishment by Israel of settlements in the Palestinian territory occupied since 1967, including East Jerusalem, has no legal validity and constitutes a flagrant violation under international law and a major obstacle to the achievement of the two-State solution and a just, lasting and comprehensive peace" (para. 1).

In the same resolution, the Security Council underlined that "it will not recognize any changes to the 4 June 1967 lines, including with regard to Jerusalem, other than those agreed by the parties through negotiations".

In paragraph 177, the Court also took note of the GA Resolution 77/126 quoted above as follows:

> 177. The principle of the prohibition of the acquisition of territory by force was equally reaffirmed by the General Assembly in several resolutions adopted with regard to the situation in the Occupied Palestinian Territory. Thus, by its resolution 77/126 of 12 December 2022, it emphasizes that "the occupation of a territory is to be a temporary, de facto situation, whereby the occupying Power can neither claim possession nor exert its sovereignty over the territory it occupies". It also recalls in this regard "the principle of the inadmissibility of the acquisition of land by force and therefore the illegality of the annexation of any part of the Occupied Palestinian Territory, including East Jerusalem, which

---

[44] UN Doc. A/77/PV.52.

[45] The 2024 ICJ Advisory Opinion, para. 176.

> constitutes a breach of international law, undermines the viability of the two-State solution and challenges the prospects for a just, lasting and comprehensive peace settlement" (para. 7).

The Court went on to dismiss the arguments relating to territorial claim of Israel by saying: 'In any event, the prohibition of the acquisition of territory by force entails that the use of force is not a means for resolving claims of sovereignty', in paragraph 178. Then, as mentioned above, in paragraph 179, the Court applied PATBF to Israel's acts in the OPT.

In the 2024 Advisory Opinion, in applying PATBF and PUF, the Court took into account the relevant Security Council and GA resolutions. As mentioned in Sect. 3.1.2, the Court did not treat the OPT as territory of a State in this Advisory Opinion. It did not make general findings on conditions for PATBF to apply to acts not taking place between States. Nevertheless, the Court admitted the application of PATBF to Israel's acts in the OPT, without considering it to be taking place between States. Therefore, the Court did not consider inter-State context as a necessary condition for applying PATBF.

It should be noted that, in admitting the application of PATBF to acts not taking place between States, the Court took into account relevant Security Council and GA resolutions supporting the application. This does not lead to the clarification of generally applicable criteria for the application of PUF or PATBF to the situation where inter-State context is lacking. On the other hand, this opinion indicates that in determining whether PUF and PATBF apply to acts not taking place between States, the views expressed by the Security Council and the GA should be taken into account. The Security Council and the GA, therefore, seem to have an important role to play in determining whether PATBF and PUF apply to acts not taking place between States.

3.3.3 Status of Territory Protected by PUF and PATBF

3.3.3.1 Internationally Recognised Territory

Article 2(4) of the UN Charter provides that all Members shall refrain in their international relations from the threat or use of force 'against the territorial integrity' or political independence of any state, or in any other manner inconsistent with the Purposes of the United Nations. As mentioned in Sects. 3.1.2 and 3.3.1 above as the Type I use of force, one of the paragraphs of the 1970 Declaration relating to PUF provides: 'Every State has the duty to refrain from the threat or use of force to violate the existing international boundaries of another State. …' In addition, the paragraph of the Declaration relating to the principle of non-acquisition of territory by force states that 'the territory of a State shall not be the object of acquisition by another State'. Therefore, it is clear that PUF applies to deployment of armed forces to another State's internationally recognised territory, and PATBF would also apply to such deployment of armed forces.

Article 3(a) of 'Definition of Aggression' annexed to United Nations General Assembly Resolution 3314 (XXIX) provides:[46]

> (a) The invasion or attack by the armed forces of a State of the territory of another State, or any military occupation, however temporary, resulting from such invasion or attack, or any annexation by the use of force of the territory of another State or part thereof,

If a State deploys armed forces to an area of another State's internationally recognised territory and takes control of the territory, it amounts to the invasion and occupation mentioned in this Article 3(a) and it is likely to violate Article 2(4) unless justified by the right to self-defence.

Article 3(e) of the 'Definition of Aggression' also refers to 'the use of armed forces of one State which are within the territory of another State with the agreement of the receiving State, in contravention of the conditions provided for in the agreement or any extension of their presence in such territory beyond the termination of the agreement'.[47] If the armed forces are deployed to another State's internationally recognised territory without the latter State's consent, regardless of the absence of violent use of force nor the absence of expression of intention to exercise sovereignty, this Article 3(e) implies that the deployment will in principle violate Article 2(4).

As an example of an attempt to acquire internationally recognised territory of another State by force, in October 2022, the GA condemned the attempted illegal annexation of four regions of Ukraine.[48] As mentioned in Chap. 1, GA resolution ES-11/4, which was adopted with 143 Member States in support, 5 against, 35 abstentions and 10 absences, refers to PUF and PATBF in its preamble, condemns Russia's 'illegal annexation' in the second operational paragraph (OP2) and declares that the attempted illegal annexation of these regions has no validity under international law in OP3. Therefore, at least 143 UN Member States seemed to consider that Russia violated PATBF through its invasion of Ukraine followed by a 'referendum' and the attempted annexation of the four regions of Ukraine.

The term 'internationally recognised territory' may have some ambiguity, but, in many cases, including the case of the four regions of Ukraine mentioned in the resolution above, whether or not an area of land has been internationally recognised as a part of a State can be determined on the basis of practices of States which have been explicitly or implicitly treating the area as a part of the State. In cases where States are taking actions to formally 'annex' land areas, such actions themselves imply that such areas have not been internationally recognised as their territory. In supporting GA resolution ES-11/4, 143 UN Member States which supported the resolution considered the four regions as Ukraine's internationally recognised territory.

The invasion of Kuwait in 1990 is another example of an attempt to acquire the internationally recognised territory of another State by force. On 9 August 1990, in

---

[46] UN Doc. A/RES/3314 (XXIX).

[47] Ruys (2014), p. 189.

[48] UN Doc. A/RES/ES-11/4, operative paragraph 2.

response to the Iraqi attempt to annex Kuwait, the Security Council adopted resolution 662. The resolution reads:[49]

> …
>
> Gravely alarmed by the declaration by Iraq of a "comprehensive and eternal merger" with Kuwait,
>
> …
>
> 1. Decides that annexation of Kuwait by Iraq under any form and whatever pretext has no legal validity, and is considered null and void;
> 2. Calls upon all States, international organizations and specialized agencies not to recognize that annexation, and to refrain from any action or dealing that might be interpreted as an indirect recognition of the annexation;
> 3. Demands that Iraq rescind its actions purporting to annex Kuwait;
> 4. Decides to keep this item on its agenda and to continue its efforts to put an early end to the occupation.

This resolution itself does not refer to PATBF, but members of the Security Council, including the United States, mentioned PATBF.[50]

3.3.3.2 'Peaceful Administration' in the Eritrea–Ethiopia Case

The Eritrea–Ethiopia Boundary Commission (EEBC) found in its Decision on Delimitation of 13 April 2002 that the town of Badme, which is located on the border between Eritrea and Ethiopia, belongs to Eritrea.[51] However, the Eritrea–Ethiopia Claims Commission (EECC) found in 2005 that Eritrea violated Article 2(4) of the UN Charter by attacking and occupying Badme in 1998. The Partial Award refers to Badme as territory that was 'peacefully administered' by Ethiopia. The relevant part of the Award reads:[52]

> 15. The areas initially invaded by Eritrean forces on that day were all either within undisputed Ethiopian territory or within territory that was peacefully administered by Ethiopia and that later would be on the Ethiopian side of the line to which Ethiopian armed forces were obligated to withdraw in 2000 under the Cease-Fire Agreement of June 18, 2000. In its Partial Award in Ethiopia's Central Front Claims, the Commission held that the best available evidence of the areas effectively administered by Ethiopia in early May 1998 is that line to which they were obligated to withdraw in 2000.

The EECC seems to be taking the position that as long as the area in question was under effective administration by Ethiopia at the time of attack, PUF may apply to Eritrea's deployment of armed forces to the area. This award did not examine how Ethiopia's administration in Badme had started and seems to be, at least partly, relying on the line of withdrawal established after the conflict by the June 2000 Ceasefire

---

[49] UN Doc. S/RES/662 (1990).

[50] Korman (1996), pp. 293–297.

[51] Eritrea-Ethiopia Boundary Commission—Decision regarding delimitation of the border between Eritrea and Ethiopia, 13 April 2002 RIIA 25 [hereinafter cited as the 2002 EEBC Decision], pp. 83–195.

[52] The 2005 EECC Partial Award, p. 467, para. 15.

Agreement, which was also a line used for the deployment of the UN Mission in Ethiopia and Eritrea (UNMEE).[53] As Sean Murphy, who was one of the counsels for Ethiopia in this case, wrote, the EECC saw the UNMEE line as most relevant in considering both *jus ad bellum* and *jus in bello* violations.[54] In this case it was not clear whether Ethiopia's administration over Badme had been peacefully established without using force. As Murphy wrote in his article, the EECC seemed to distinguish between Ethiopia's *de facto* administration before 1998 and Eritrea's occupation after 1998. He wrote: 'Eritrea could not use force to seize disputed territory it regarded as illegally occupied by Ethiopia, when Ethiopia had administered that territory for many years. By contrast, Ethiopia could use force as necessary and proportionate to reclaim territory it regarded as illegally occupied by Eritrea, so long as it did so shortly after Eritrea seized the territory by force.' He further wrote: 'Article 2(4) only precludes a State from using force to seize control of disputed territory that has been peacefully administered by another State for a long period of time'.[55] Ethiopia's use of force against Eritrea was not regarded as violation of Article 2(4).

The 'peaceful administration' mentioned in the EECC Partial Award does not mean that Ethiopia's administration had been 'established' peacefully. In the Eritrea–Ethiopia case, it was not clear when and how Ethiopia's administration over Badme was established, and, after Eritrea gained independence from Ethiopia in 1993, Eritrea seemed to have started to protest to Ethiopia about the latter's claims to sovereignty over parts of Eritrea's territory and of using force and threats to pursue these claims.[56] Therefore, 'peaceful administration' here should mean *de facto* administration of Badme by Ethiopia for 5 years from 1993 to 1998 which might have been protested by Eritrea but not physically challenged.

A Comprehensive Peace Agreement signed by Ethiopia and Eritrea on 12 December 2000 (the Algiers Agreement) provided for the establishment of three dispute settlement bodies.[57] Article 4 created the EEBC to delimit and demarcate the boundary based on pertinent colonial treaties and applicable international law. Article 5 set up the EECC to arbitrate claims for loss, damage or injury by one government against the other and by nationals of one party against the government of the other. Article 3 provided for the establishment of an independent body under OAU auspices to carry out an investigation 'to determine the origins of the conflict' but this body was never established, and when and how Ethiopia's administration was established over Badme was not clarified.[58]

---

[53] The 2005 EECC Partial Award, p. 467, para. 15, Eritrea-Ethiopia Claims Commission—Partial Award: Central Front—Ethiopia's Claim 2, 28 April 2004, RIIA 26 [herein after cited as 2006 EECC Partial Award], para. 27. See Gray (2006), pp. 710–711.

[54] Murphy (2018), p. 568.

[55] Ibid. p. 570.

[56] Gray (2006). p. 718.

[57] https://unmee.unmissions.org/algiers-peace-agreement

[58] Gray (2006), p. 703.

If State A has been administering an area of land for 5 years, and State B has been protesting to State A's administration, but it has not physically challenged the administration, this *de facto* administration for 5 years seems to satisfy the definition of 'peaceful administration' mentioned in the 2005 EECC Partial Award.[59] According to the logic adopted by the EECC, this 'peaceful administration' may be sufficient for making State B's deployment of armed force to the territory under State A's *de facto* administration likely to violate PUF, unless State A has attacked State B and State B can justify its use of force based on the right to self-defence.[60]

As mentioned as the Type II use of force in Sects. 3.1.2 and 3.3.1 above, the 1970 Declaration provides that: 'Such a threat or use of force constitutes a violation of international law and the Charter of the United Nations and shall never be employed as a means of settling international issues. ... Every State has the duty to refrain from the threat or use of force ... as a means of solving international disputes, including territorial disputes and problems concerning frontiers of States'. The approach taken by the EECC seems to be consistent with this part of the 1970 Declaration. In addition, the Security Council resolution 1177 adopted on 16 June 1998 in response to the Eritrea–Ethiopia conflict also affirmed the Type II use of force. Relevant parts of this resolution read:[61]

> Affirming the principle of peaceful settlement of disputes and stressing that the use of armed force is not acceptable as a means of addressing territorial disputes or changing circumstances on the ground,
>
> ...
>
> 1. Condemns the use of force and demands that both parties immediately cease hostilities and refrain from further use of force;
> 2. Welcomes the commitment of the parties to a moratorium on the threat of and use of air strikes;
> 3. Urges the parties to exhaust all means to achieve a peaceful settlement of the dispute; ...

The prohibition of use of force against 'peacefully administrated' territory, which was advocated by the EECC, contributes to upholding the principle of peaceful settlement of disputes. Therefore, as the Type II use of force, State B's deployment of armed forces above may amount to a violation of PUF, unless State A has attacked State B and State B can justify its use of force based on the right to self-defence.[62]

---

[59] Klein and Koutroulis (2018), p. 259.

[60] Gray analysed this logic critically (Gray 2006). Murphy accepted it (Murphy (2018). Ruys seems to indicate that, if a State's 'peaceful administration' over territory has been established unlawfully, and the real owner of its sovereignty takes back control through the use of force, the use of force to take back the control might amount to the violation of the prohibition of use of force, but State responsibility can be offset, with reference to Article 39 of the ILC Articles on State Responsibility, by allowing it to maintain the control. (Ruys (2021) International Law Studies, pp. 719–720).

[61] UN Doc. S/RES/1177(1998).

[62] This does not mean that this 'peaceful administration' is a precondition for applying the prohibition of the Type II use of force to territory subject to competing claims, but the existence of 'peaceful administration' contributes to the violation of the prohibition. As will be mentioned in Sect.

Regarding the deploying State's invocation of right to self-defence, the EECC denied the invocation of the right to self-defence by Eritrea. The EECC said:

> It is true that the boundary between Eritrea and Ethiopia in the area of Badme was never marked in the years when Eritrea was an Italian colony, during Eritrea's subsequent incorporation into Ethiopia, or after Eritrean independence in 1993, and it is clear that the Parties had differing conceptions of the boundary's location.

However, it concluded by saying that 'localized border encounters between small infantry units' did not constitute an armed attack and by also mentioning Eritrea's failure to report to the Security Council. In applying PUF the existence of justification based on the right to self-defence must be examined, and the next section will address this issue in more detail.

3.3.3.3 Absence of Justification for the Deployment of Armed Forces

To apply the prohibition of Type II use of force to State B's deployment of armed forces to an area of land under State A's *de facto* administration, the absence of justification for State B's use of force must be confirmed. If State B invokes the right to self-defence by showing credible evidence of an armed attack by State A, third States should look at it carefully and determine if the evidence of an armed attack is plausible. On 24 February 2022, when Russia started a full-scale invasion of Ukraine, Russian President Putin made a speech referring to the right to collective self-defence under Article 51 of the UN Charter for the two 'Republics' of Donetsk and Lugansk.[63] President Putin argued:

> In this context, in accordance with Article 51 (Chapter VII) of the UN Charter, with permission of Russia's Federation Council, and in execution of the treaties of friendship and mutual assistance with the Donetsk People's Republic and the Lugansk People's Republic, ratified by the Federal Assembly on February 22, I made a decision to carry out a special military operation.

On 7 March 2022, Russia sent a document to the ICJ denying the ICJ's jurisdiction on the case instituted by Ukraine under the Genocide Convention. This document reads:[64]

> 15. The special military operation conducted by Russia in the territory of Ukraine is based on the United Nations Charter, its Article 51 and customary international law. The legal basis for the military operation was communicated on 24 February 2022 to the Secretary-

3.4.5 below, in 2015, Judge Owada and Judge Robinson of the ICJ took the position that Nicaragua's deployment of armed forces to territory under dispute with Costa Rica violated PUS, but the territory in question did not seem to be under Costa Rica's 'peaceful administration' in the sense of the term used by the EECC.

[63] Address by the President of the Russian Federation, 24 February 2022, http://en.kremlin.ru/events/president/news/67843

[64] Document (with annexes) from the Russian Federation setting out its position regarding alleged "lack of jurisdiction" of the Court in the case, 7 March 2022. https://www.icj-cij.org/sites/default/files/case-related/182/182-20220307-OTH-01-00-EN.pdf

> General of the United Nations and the United Nations Security Council by the Permanent Representative of the Russian Federation to the United Nations in the form of a notification under Article 51 of the United Nations Charter. The relevant letter addressed to the UN Secretary-General with the request to circulate it as a document of the UN Security Council forwarded "the address of the President of the Russian Federation H.E. Mr. Vladimir Putin to the citizens of Russia informing them of the measures taken in accordance with Article 51 of the UN Charter in exercise of the right of self-defense" (attached).

The communication from Russia to the Security Council through the UN Secretary-General on 24 February 2022 consists of a short cover letter from Russian Permanent Representative to the UN and a copy of the President Putin's speech on the same date. The cover letter reads:[65]

> I have the honour to forward herewith the text of the address of the President of the Russian Federation, Vladimir Putin, to the citizens of Russia, informing them of the measures taken in accordance with Article 51 of the Charter of the United Nations in exercise of the right of self-defence (see annex). I would ask you to circulate the present letter and its annex as a document of the Security Council.

However, there is no reference to any armed attack by Ukraine in his speech nor in documents accompanying it in these communications. If Russia relies on the right to collective self-defence under Article 51, it must at least try to show the existence of an armed attack. If it does not, it cannot justify its full-scale invasion into the neighbouring State. In this case, the invocation of the right to collective self-defence clearly lacks its very basic pre-condition.[66]

In the case of the Second Nagorno-Karabakh War in 2020, the possibility of the invocation of the right to self-defence by Azerbaijan was debated among scholars.[67] In this case, there were strong cases for and against Azerbaijan's invocation of the right to self-defence, mainly due to the long interval between the First Nagorno-Karabakh War (1988–1994) and the Second Nagorno-Karabakh War (2020).

Akande and Tzanakopoulos wrote on this case that the distinction needs to be drawn between 'an outstanding territorial dispute where no force (or at least no unlawful force in the post-Charter period) has yet been used by any of the disputing parties' and 'a situation where one state creates (or escalates) a territorial dispute by unlawfully invading and occupying territory held by another state'.[68] They argue that '[w]hile no force can be used by either party in the former instance, the latter instance is clearly one where an armed attack has taken place and the right of self-defence is, in the first instance at the very least, triggered'. Distinction between these two situations mentioned by Akande and Tzanakopoulos is not always very clear,[69] but, whether there was an armed attack by a State against another in the post-WWII period might not be impossible to examine. Akande and Tzanakopoulos

[65] UN Doc. S/2022/154.

[66] For more detailed examination of Russia's possible justification, see Asada (2024), pp. 4–11.

[67] Ruys and Silvestre (2021a EJIL), Akande and Tzanakopoulos (2021 EJIL), Ruys and Silvestre (2021b International Law Studies).

[68] Akande and Tzanakopoulos (2021). p. 1302.

[69] Ruys and Silvestre (2021a EJIL), p. 1293.

argued, in some cases an armed attack may continue in the form of occupation. If State A is administering an area of land, it is necessary for third States to look at the origin of the administration going back to the time when the use of force became unlawful under international law. If State A started occupation through an armed attack against State B which was administering the area, State B might be able to resort to use of force based on its right to self-defence. It might be difficult for third States to determine if State B can invoke right to self-defence, but third States can at least examine if there was an armed attack under Article 51 of the UN Charter which may justify the invocation of the right to self-defence.

In addition to the right to self-defence against an armed attack under Article 51 of the UN Charter, in the 2004 Wall Advisory Opinion the ICJ referred to 'the right, and indeed the duty, to respond in order to protect the life of its citizens'. After concluding that Article 51 does not apply in paragraph 139 of the opinion, the ICJ added in paragraph 141:[70]

> 141. The fact remains that Israel has to face numerous indiscriminate and deadly acts of violence against its civilian population. It has the right, and indeed the duty, to respond in order to protect the life of its citizens. The measures taken are bound nonetheless to remain in conformity with applicable international law.

This right and duty to respond in order to protect citizens can be a factor justifying the deployment of armed forces, for example, if the citizens are facing violence emanating from the territory in question.

As will be examined in Sect. 4.1.4 below, even if State B's initial deployment may be justified by its right to self-defence, in cases where PATBF applies to the deployment, once State B starts to annex the area, it may violate both PATBF and PUF. Therefore, when PATBF applies, the right to self-defence may not be able to justify State B's attempt to acquire territory. On the other hand, in cases where it is not clear whether PATBF applies, as mentioned in Sect. 3.1.2 above, the prohibition of the Type II use of force may be easier to apply for third States as an alternative rule of international law against potential attempts to acquire territory by force. However, in applying the prohibition of the Type II use of force, third States need to examine whether the deployment of armed forces is justified by the right to self-defence, or the right and duty to respond in order to protect citizens mentioned in the 2004 Wall Advisory Opinion.

3.3.3.4 Peacefully 'Established' Administration

The deployment of armed forces to an area of land under State A's 'peacefully administrated' territory, in the sense of the 2005 EECC Partial Award mentioned in Sect. 3.3.3.2, may violate the prohibition of the Type II use of force. On the other hand, if State A has not used force in establishing the administration and has peacefully 'established' administration without protest from State B, in view of the

[70] The 2004 ICJ Wall Advisory Opinion, para. 141.

peaceful nature of the establishment of administration, it is likely to deserve even stronger protection by the prohibition of the Type II use of force which advocates the principle of peaceful settlement of disputes.

When a State intends to exercise sovereignty over an area of land, it would take measures regulating the activities in the area to put it under effective control. In the context of territorial disputes, the ICJ often considers 'acts and activities considered to be performed *à titre de souverain'* or *effectivités* as evidence of establishment of sovereignty. According to the Court, such acts include, 'in particular, but not limited to, legislative acts or acts of administrative control, acts relating to the application and enforcement of criminal or civil law, acts regulating immigration, acts regulating fishing and other economic activities, naval patrols as well as search and rescue operations'.[71] These are primarily measures regulating the activities of people in the territory, and they are taken to establish administration. In this book, such measures are broadly referred to as 'administrative measures'.

The peacefulness of the establishment of administration would be strengthened if administrative measures are taken not only without use of force or coercion but also without protest from other claimants. If State A openly and constantly[72] conducts administrative measures regulating activities of people in an area of land for a period much longer than 5 years in the Eritrea–Ethiopia case without using force or coercion against another claimant, State B, and without receiving any protest from State B, State A's administration should be deemed peacefully established for that period. If there is a treaty between State A and State B clearly referring to the area as State B's territory, State A's administrative measures would violate the treaty and would not be truly peaceful. Therefore, peacefully established administration here implies that such a treaty does not exist. If the period of peacefully established administration is 20 years, this case would look as follows.

Case 1.0 State A has been openly and constantly taking administrative measures regulating the activities of people in an area of land for 20 years. State B has not been in national emergency or other conditions which hinders it to take measures relating to the territory, but it has not protested to State A's administration. There is no treaty between State A and State B clearly referring to the area as State B's territory, and during the 20 years State A did not notice State B's administrative measures regulating activities in the area.

In Case 1.0, in establishing the administration, State A has been taking peaceful measures without resorting to use of force or coercion and without receiving protest

[71] Territorial and Maritime Dispute (Nicaragua v Columbia), Judgment, 19 November 2012, ICJ Rep. (2012) [hereinafter cited as the Nicaragua v Columbia judgment], para. 80. Territorial and Maritime Dispute between Nicaragua and Honduras in the Caribbean Sea (Nicaragua v Honduras), Judgment, 8 October 2007, ICJ Rep. (2007) [hereinafter cited as the Nicaragua v Honduras judgment], pp. 713–722, paras. 176–208.

[72] The term 'constantly' is admittedly ambiguous. The administrative measures required for maintaining effective control over an area of land depends on each situation, and the term 'constantly' here means as frequently as necessary for maintaining effective control.

from State B. This peaceful nature of the establishment of administration should deserve stronger protection from the perspective of upholding the principle of peaceful settlement of disputes than the administration in the Eritrea–Ethiopia case which might have been established through use of force or coercion and has been protested within 5 years. Therefore, the deployment of armed forces to territory under peacefully 'established' administration for 20 years in Case 1.0 is even likelier to violate the prohibition of the Type II use of force than the deployment of armed forces to territory under 'peaceful administration' in the sense of the 2005 EECC Partial Award.

The application of PATBF to territory subject to competing claims was preliminarily examined in Sect. 3.1.2. As mentioned in Sect. 3.3.3.1 above, the paragraph of the1970 Declaration relating to PATBF is clear about the application of the prohibition to internationally recognised territory. On the other hand, the last sentence of the paragraph provides: 'No territorial acquisition resulting from the threat or use of force shall be recognized as legal'. This sentence does not explicitly limit 'the threat or use of force' to threat or use of force against another State's territory, and in the 2024 Advisory Opinion the ICJ applied PATBF to Israel's acts in the OPT, which was not treated by the ICJ as a territory of a State. In Case 1.0, 20 years of State A's open and constant administrative measures may provide evidence of acts and activities considered to be performed *à titre de souverain* or *effectivité* for consolidating territorial title. On the other hand, while there is no treaty between State A and State B clearly referring to the area as State B's territory, there might be a treaty or agreement which ambiguously refers to the area and could provide evidence for State B's territorial title. In addition, while State A did not notice State B's administrative measures during the 20 years, it does not exclude the possibility that State B had taken some administrative measures before State A started open and constant administrative measures. Therefore, the relative strength of State A's territorial title is not clear in Case 1.0, and, if the strict understanding of PATBF, which requires State A's territorial title to be at least as strong as State B's to apply PATBF to State B, is adopted, it is not clear if PATBF applies to State B in Case 1.0.

On the other hand, if, during the 20 years of State A's peacefully established administration, government officials of State B have become aware of State A's administrative measures in the area, but it has not protested about them, this additional factor should strengthen State A's position against State B.

Case 1.1 State A has been openly and constantly taking administrative measures regulating the activities of people in an area of land for 20 years. State B has not been in national emergency or other conditions which hinders it to take measures relating to the territory. State B has become aware of State A's administrative measures but has not protested to State A. There is no treaty between State A and State B clearly referring to the area as State B's territory.

If State B has become aware of State A's administrative measures but has not protested to State A, the absence of reaction might amount to acquiescence to State A's sovereignty, which passes one State's existing sovereignty over an area to another State even when the former State had sovereignty over the territory before the acquiescence. In the Judgment on the Sovereignty over the Pedra Branca/ Pulau Batu Puteh, Middle Rocks and South Ledge (Malaysia v. Singapore) case, the ICJ clarified the concept of acquiescence in the context of territorial dispute. The relevant part of the judgment reads:[73]

> 121. Under certain circumstances, sovereignty over territory might pass as a result of the failure of the State which has sovereignty to respond to conduct *à titre de souverain* of the other State or, as Judge Huber put it in the Island of Palmas case, to concrete manifestations of the display of territorial sovereignty by the other State *(Island of Palmas Case (Netherlands/United States of America), Award of 4 April 1928, RIAA, Vol. II, (1949) p. 839)*. Such manifestations of the display of sovereignty may call for a response if they are not to be opposable to the State in question. The absence of reaction may well amount to acquiescence. The concept of acquiescence
>
> > "is equivalent to tacit recognition manifested by unilateral conduct which the other party may interpret as consent ..." *(Delimitation of the Maritime Boundary in the Gulf of Maine Area (Canada/United States of America), Judgment, I.C.J. Reports 1984, p. 305, para. 130)*
>
> That is to say, silence may also speak, but only if the conduct of the other State calls for a response.
>
> 122. Critical for the Court's assessment of the conduct of the Parties is the central importance in international law and relations of State sovereignty over territory and of the stability and certainty of that sovereignty. Because of that, any passing of sovereignty over territory on the basis of the conduct of the Parties, as set out above, must be manifested clearly and without any doubt by that conduct and the relevant facts. That is especially so if what may be involved, in the case of one of the Parties, is in effect the abandonment of sovereignty over part of its territory.

State B's failure to protest to State A's administrative measures would, even if it does not amount to acquiescence, significantly strengthen State A's position against State B and make it difficult for State B to argue that it honestly believed it had stronger territorial title based on international law than State A. Therefore, while the application of PATBF requires case-by-case analysis, in Case 1.1, even if the strict understanding of PATBF above is adopted, there is at least a possibility that a third-party dispute settlement body like the ICJ may, if referred to it in the future, find the violation of PATBF by State B's deployment of armed forces to the territory under State A's peacefully established administration for 20 years. In addition, the additional factor in Case 1.1 would also strengthen the peaceful nature of State A's establishment of administration in relation to State B and make State B's deployment of armed forces in Case 1.1 even likelier to violate the prohibition of Type II use of force than in Case 1.0.

The G7 Foreign Ministers' Communiqué of 18 April 2023 mentioned in Chap. 1 declared that PATBF should be observed in good faith and strongly opposed any unilateral attempts to change the 'peacefully established status of territories by force or coercion'. The relevant part of the Communiqué reads:

---

[73] Sovereignty over Pedra Branca/ Pulau Batu Puteh, Middle Rocks and South Ledge (Malaysia v. Singapore), Judgement, 23 May 2008, ICJ Rep. (2008) [hereinafter cited as the Pedra Branca judgment], paras. 121–122.

> The prohibition of threats or the use of force against the territorial integrity or political independence of any state, in accordance with the provisions of the UN Charter, constitutes the cornerstone of the post-war international system. Yet, territorial ambition is again driving some states to return to rule by force, so we have redoubled our efforts to uphold peace guided by the rule of law. The prohibition on the acquisition of territory resulting from the threat or use of force, reaffirmed in the Friendly Relations Declaration of 1970, should be observed in good faith. We strongly oppose any unilateral attempts to change the peacefully established status of territories by force or coercion anywhere in the world. In this regard, sending regular or irregular forces to unilaterally annex a territory is prohibited.

As will be examined in Sect. 4.2, the violation of PATBF leads to the obligation for third States, and third States should take a precautionary approach in recognising the State B's annexation of the area in question. Real situations might be more complicated than these hypothetical cases and it might not be easy for third States to take a position on relevant facts. However, if there is a situation like Case 1.1 above, third States should make efforts to analyse available evidence as much as possible.

3.3.3.5 Peacefully Established Administration for a Longer Period

In 1928, Max Huber famously wrote as the arbitrator in the Arbitral Award on the Island of Palmas case that 'peaceful and continuous display' of territorial sovereignty leads to a territorial title. The relevant part of the Award reads:[74]

> So true is this, that practice, as well as doctrine, recognises – though under different legal formulae and with certain differences as to the conditions required – that the continuous and peaceful display of territorial sovereignty (peaceful in relation to other States) is as good as a title. ... If the effectiveness has above all been insisted on in regard to occupation, this is because the question rarely arises in connection with territories in which there is already an established order of things. Just as before the rise of international law, boundaries of lands were necessarily determined by the fact that the power of a State was exercised within them, so too, under the reign of international law, the fact of peaceful and continuous display is still one of the most important considerations in establishing boundaries between States.

In the Ligitan and Sipadan case, the ICJ observed that the dispute did not crystallise until 1969.[75] Malaysia presented the measures taken by the North Borneo authorities to regulate and control the collecting of turtle eggs on Ligitan and Sipadan based on the Turtle Preservation Ordinance of 1917 as evidence of effective administration (*effectivités*) over the islands. Malaysia presented evidence of *effectivités* covering a period until the 1960s.[76] In the 2002 Ligitan and Sipadan judgment, the Court concluded that activities including these measures 'cover a considerable period of time' and reveal 'an intention to exercise State functions in respect of the

---

[74] The Island of Palmas Case (USA v. The Netherlands), Award of the Tribunal, 4 April 1928, RIAA 2, p. 839.

[75] Case Concerning Sovereignty over Pulau Ligitan and Pulau Sipadan (Indonesia v Malaysia), Judgment, 17 December 2002, ICJ Rep. (2002) [hereinafter cited as the Ligitan and Sipadan judgment], paras. 128–129, 135.

[76] Ibid. para. 143.

two islands'.[77] The Court also said: 'The Court moreover cannot disregard the fact that at the time when these activities were carried out, neither Indonesia nor its predecessor, the Netherlands, ever expressed its disagreement or protest'.[78] In the Ligitan and Sipadan judgment, the ICJ mentioned the absence of protest from the Indonesian side for 'a considerable period of time' in determining Malaysia's sovereignty over the islands. In this case the length of a 'considerable period of time' was about 50 years.

In Case 1.0 above, State A did not notice State B's administrative measures during the 20 years, but it does not exclude the possibility that State B had taken some administrative measures before State A started open and constant administrative measures. In addition, it does not exclude the possibility that there exists an ambiguous treaty or agreement possibly supporting State B's territorial title. On the other hand, if State A's open and constant administrative measures have continued for 50 years without protest from State B, as the ICJ said in the Ligitan and Sipadan judgment, the fact that State B never expressed its protest at the time when State A's administrative measures were openly carried out cannot be disregarded.[79] Unless there are facts justifying the absence of protest for 50 years or convincing treaty-based evidence proving a territorial title preceding State A's peaceful administration for 50 years, this peacefully established administration for 50 years without protest from State B seems likely to indicate State A's superior territorial title. If State B has also been taking administrative measures, it should have noticed State A's administrative measures, and, if it has noticed them, it should have protested about them. The absence of State B's protest for 50 years, therefore, casts serious doubt on State B's will to exercise sovereignty over the area. While there might be no evidence showing State B's actual knowledge of State A's administrative measures, if State B had a will to exercise sovereignty over the area, it should have paid attention to the area and noticed State A's constant administrative measures for 'a considerable period of time' like 50 years in the Lilgitan and Sipadan case. Therefore, State A's

---

[77] Ibid. para. 148.

[78] Ibid.

[79] Peaceful occupation of 20 years is sufficient for acquisitive prescription or adverse possession of land property under domestic laws. Acquisitive prescription or adverse possession of land property often requires open and notorious use of another owner's land for a continuous and uninterrupted period of 10–20 years. As an example of provisions on acquisitive prescription, Article 162 of the Japanese Civil Code provides:

Section 2 Acquisitive Prescription

Acquisitive Prescription of Ownership
Article 162

(1)A person that possesses the property of another for 20 years peacefully and openly with the intention to own it acquires ownership thereof.

(2)A person that possesses the property of another for 10 years peacefully and openly with an intention to own it acquires ownership thereof if the person was acting in good faith and was not negligent at the time when the possession started.

(See also Britannica.com https://www.britannica.com/money/prescription-property-law).

open and constant administrative measures and State B's failure to protest for such a long period would make it difficult to believe that State B honestly believed in having stronger territorial title based on international law than State A. Therefore, while the application of PATBF requires case-by-case analysis, State B's deployment of armed forces to territory under State A's peacefully established administration for such a long period would have the possibility of violating PATBF. In addition, these factors strengthen the peaceful nature of State A's administration and would also make State B's deployment of armed forces to the territory very likely to violate the prohibition of the Type II use of force.

It might not be easy for third States to take a position on the relevant facts, especially when, as in the case of the Ligitan and Sipadan case, evidence of administration is not very strong nor numerous. However, if there is clear evidence of open and constant administrative measures, it would not be impossible for them to make objective assessment without waiting for the decision by the ICJ or other legally binding dispute settlement mechanisms. Where there are strong indicators of consolidation of territorial title, they need to look at available information and take a precautionary approach in avoiding premature and possibly unlawful recognition of the situation created by the deployment of armed forces. Third States should look at the evidence shown by State A and State B and consider if it is plausible that State A's administration has been peacefully established without resorting to use of force and without receiving protest from State B for a considerable period like 50 years.

3.3.3.6 Treaty-Based Territorial Title

As mentioned above, even when there is no treaty between State A and State B clearly referring to the area as State B's territory, there might be an ambiguous treaty or agreement which could provide evidence for State B's territorial title. A State can acquire territory through an agreement with relevant actors and subsequent practice relating to its implementation, as Costa Rica and Cameroon did in the Costa Rica v Nicaragua case[80] and the Case Concerning the Land and Maritime Boundary between Cameroon and Nigeria[81] respectively, and as Eritrea did in the Eritrea–Ethiopia case.[82] However, as these cases indicate, relevant agreements and subsequent practice tend to be difficult for third States to interpret without the help of third-party bodies, particularly because they are not parties to these agreements. Furthermore, as will be explained in the next section, the ICJ did not find the violation of PUF by Nicaragua nor Nigeria in these cases, and PATBF was not mentioned in the respective judgments. The absence of a finding on these issues might indicate that the ambiguity of treaty-based territorial title in these cases at the time of deploy-

[80] The Costa Rica v Nicaragua judgment, pp. 700–703, paras. 76, 89, 92.

[81] Land and Maritime Boundary between Cameroon and Nigeria (Cameroon v Nigeria: Equatorial Guinea intervening), Judgment, 10 October 2002, ICJ Rep. (2002) [hereinafter cited as Cameroon v Nigeria judgment], p.416, para. 225.

[82] See Sect. 3.3.1 above.

ment of armed forces has made it difficult to apply PUF and PATBF. Therefore, if the deploying State presents credible evidence relating to a treaty which may give it a territorial title to the territory in question, third States should look at it carefully.

On the other hand, if the territory in question has been under peacefully established administration of State A for 20 years as in Case 1.0 in Sect. 3.3.3.4, PUF should protect State A's administration against State B's Type II use of force. If there is evidence showing that State B has become aware of State A's administration but did not protest as in Case 1.1, third States should also examine if State B's failure to protest may amount to acquiescence to State A's sovereignty over the territory in question. If State A has been peacefully administering the territory for a longer period like 50 years without protest from State B, the longstanding peaceful administration deserves stronger protection against State B's Type II use of force, and the absence of protest for 50 years calls for particularly cautious examination of the evidence relating to the alleged treaty-based territorial title presented by State B.

3.3.4 Resort to Use of Force Despite Available Third-Party Mechanism

In the Cameroon v Nigeria case, the Nigerian army was deployed to Lake Chad area and Bakassi Peninsula, which were disputed with Cameroon. In this case the ICJ found that 'the Federal Republic of Nigeria is under an obligation expeditiously and without condition to withdraw its administration and its military and police forces from the territories which fall within the sovereignty of the Republic of Cameroon',[83] but avoided making a finding on the violation of Article 2(4) as follows:

> 319. In the circumstances of the case, the Court considers moreover that, by the very fact of the present Judgment and of the evacuation of the Cameroonian territory occupied by Nigeria, the injury suffered by Cameroon by reason of the occupation of its territory will in all events have been sufficiently addressed. The Court will not therefore seek to ascertain whether and to what extent Nigeria's responsibility to Cameroon has been engaged as a result of that occupation.

In the Costa Rica v Nicaragua case, Nicaragua established a military presence in the disputed territory. In its judgment of 16 December 2015, the ICJ found: 'Costa Rica has sovereignty over the "disputed territory" as defined by the Court'.[84] Costa Rica asked the ICJ to find that Nicaragua breached Article 2(4), but the ICJ avoided making a finding on this issue as follows:[85]

> ...in the circumstances, given that the unlawful character of these activities has already been established, the Court need not dwell any further on this submission. As in the case concerning Land and Maritime Boundary between Cameroon and Nigeria (Cameroon v.

[83] The Cameroon v Nigeria judgment, p. 457, para. 325. V.(A).

[84] The Costa Rica v Nicaragua judgment, p. 740, para. 229.

[85] Ibid. p. 704, para. 97.

> Nigeria Equatorial Guinea intervening), the Court finds that 'by the very fact of the present Judgment and of the evacuation' of the disputed territory, the injury suffered by Costa Rica 'will in all events have been sufficiently addressed'.

In both the Cameroon v Nigeria case and the Costa Rica v Nicaragua case, the ICJ had jurisdiction over the territorial disputes and Nigeria and Nicaragua were ordered to withdraw from the area of land which belonged to Cameroon and Costa Rica respectively, and the disputes were resolved through the judicial proceedings. Other factors, including Nigeria's plea of honest mistake, low intensity of Nicaragua's deployment of armed force, and, possibly, the ambiguity of Cameroon and Costa Rica's treaty-based territorial title at the time of the deployment of armed forces might have contributed to the ICJ's decision not to render findings on the violation of PUF. However, in these cases, the ICJ said 'by the very fact of the present judgment' the injury suffered has been sufficiently addressed, and the availability of these binding settlements on the territorial disputes also seems to have contributed to the ICJ's decision not to embark on the finding on the violation of PUF.

As in these two cases, when the State deploying the armed forces to the territory in question is accepting the jurisdiction of ICJ or other third-party dispute settlement mechanisms through declaration under Article 36(2) of the ICJ Statute or other international agreements to which the deploying State and the other claimants are the parties, the territorial dispute can be resolved through these legal mechanisms. If the deploying State is accepting the ICJ's jurisdiction but other claimants do not accept it, the ICJ cannot exercise its jurisdiction. In such a situation the other claimants which are not accepting the ICJ's jurisdiction should also deposit declarations under Article 36(2) of the ICJ Statute and bring the case before the ICJ. On the other hand, if the deploying State is not making declarations under Article 36(2) of the ICJ Statute accepting jurisdiction for dispute relating to territory and use of force, but the other claimants are doing so, there is no available third-party dispute settlement based on international law. In this case, the deploying State is choosing the deployment of armed forces as a means of settling an international issue despite the existence of an available legal dispute settlement mechanism.

This choice of use of armed forces as a means of settling an international issue despite the availability of the ICJ as a means of settlement, would make the deployment a more serious Type II use of force than the deployment of armed forces in cases where such means of settlement are or become available as in the Cameroon v Nigeria and Costa Rica v Nicaragua cases. Article 2(3) of the UN Charter provides:

> All Members shall settle their international disputes by peaceful means in such a manner that international peace and security, and justice, are not endangered.

The 'Manila Declaration on the Peaceful Settlement of Disputes between States' (the Manila Declaration) was adopted by the General Assembly on 15 November 1982 by consensus,[86] and this declaration is an important document showing the view of the UN Member States on the principle of peaceful settlement under Article

[86] UN Doc. A/RES/37/10. Tomuschat (2024) (Article 2(3)), p. 269, Shinkaretskaia (1989) pp. 48–9.

2(3) of the UN Charter. The preamble of the Manila Declaration reaffirmed 'the need to exert utmost efforts in order to settle any conflicts and disputes between States exclusively by peaceful means and to avoid any military action and hostilities'. This preamble clarifies the two aspects of the obligation under Article 2(3) by stating that States not only have a positive obligation to do their utmost to settle disputes by peaceful means but they also have a negative obligation not to resort to any military action and hostilities. The word 'exclusively' in the operative paragraph 2 of the Manila Declaration also seems to support this latter aspect. The OP2 provides as follows:

> Every State shall settle its international dispute exclusively by peaceful means in such a manner that international peace and security, and justice, are not endangered.

The deployment of armed forces to the territory subject to competing claims without accepting the ICJ's jurisdiction over the issues relating to the territory, while the other claimant is accepting the ICJ's jurisdiction, would not be consistent with the obligation to settle the dispute exclusively by peaceful means and not to resort to military action. As mentioned above, on the application of PUF to territory subject to competing claims by States, Corten pointed out 'the need to interpret article 2(4) in conjunction with article 2(3)'.[87] Article 2(3) provides an important context for the interpretation of Article 2(4). This choice of use of force as a means of settling an international issue, despite the availability of the ICJ as a means of settlement, would make the deployment more serious and difficult to resolve than in the Nigeria v Cameroon case or Costa Rica v Nicaragua case, and this deployment is likelier to violate the obligation to settle the dispute peacefully under Article 2(3) of the Charter than Nigeria and Nicaragua in these cases. As Article 2(4) needs to be interpreted in conjunction with Article 2(3), particularly in applying the prohibition of the Type II use of force in the 1970 Declaration, this violation of Article 2(3) should contribute to the violation of PUF.

Article 33(1) of the UN Charter provides:

> The parties to any dispute, the continuance of which is likely to endanger the maintenance of international peace and security, shall, first of all, seek a solution by negotiation, enquiry, mediation, conciliation, arbitration, judicial settlement, resort to regional agencies or arrangements, or other peaceful means of their own choice.

The last part of Article 33(1) is often called 'free choice of means'.[88] Action 17 of the Pact for the Future also refers to the last part of Article 33(1), but, compared with Article 33(1), Action 17 of the Pact puts more emphasis on the role of the ICJ. The relevant part reads as follows:[89]

> We recognize the positive contribution of the International Court of Justice, the principal judicial organ of the United Nations, including in adjudicating disputes among States. We

[87] Corten (2010), p. 149.

[88] Tomuschat (2024) (Article 33), p. 1421.

[89] UN Doc. A/79/1.

> reaffirm the obligation of all States to comply with the decisions of the International Court of Justice in cases to which they are parties. We decide to:
> (a) Take appropriate steps to ensure that the International Court of Justice can fully and effectively discharge its mandate and promote awareness of its role in the peaceful settlement of disputes, while respecting that parties to any dispute may also seek other peaceful means of their own choice.

The last part of Article 33(1) must be read in conjunction with Article 2(3) and Article 2(4). If a State resorts to means involving armed forces in settling dispute, offers negotiation as the only means of settlement and denies the third-party dispute settlement mechanism based on international law which is accepted by the other party, in particular the ICJ, which all the UN Member States accept as the principal judicial organ of the UN under Article 92 of the UN Charter, it cannot claim to be exerting utmost efforts to settle the dispute peacefully, and its resort to use of armed forces would violate Article 2(3). As Article 2(3) constitutes an important context for the interpretation of Article 2(4), this violation of Article 2(3) should contribute to the violation of the prohibition of Type II use of force.

3.4 Acts Involving Use of Force

3.4.1 Use of Armed Force

Whether 'force' in Article 2(4) includes economic force has been controversial. During the San Francisco Conference in 1945, the proposal of the Brazilian delegate to include 'the threat or use of economic measures' under Article 2(4) was rejected by the drafting committee.[90] Pobjie examined the meaning of 'use of force' in her book in detail, and she examined whether 'force' in Article 2(4) is restricted to physical/armed force only. After examining the debates on this subject in the drafting of the 1970 Declarations, she concluded that ultimately there was no subsequent agreement overturning the drafter's clear intent on this point.[91] She also wrote:[92]

> Despite some earlier scholarly view, the position that 'force' in article 2(4) includes only armed/physical force and excludes other forms of non-armed coercion is today overwhelmingly supported by scholars.

Tams also quotes the jurisprudence of the ICJ which appears to imply that the use of force under Article 2(4) is limited to armed force and concludes:[93]

---

[90] Corten (2010), p. 54. Dörr and Randelzhofer (2012), p. 209. Pobjie (2024), p. 117. Tams (2024), p. 310.

[91] Pobjie (2024), pp. 117, 124.

[92] Ibid. p. 125.

[93] Tams (2024), p. 311.

> Reflecting the combined effects of the Friendly Relations Declaration and ICJ pronouncements, this view has by now become generally accepted.

Therefore, the use of 'armed' force should be considered a pre-condition for the application of PUF and its corollary PATBF.

On the other hand, 'armed' force is not limited to regular military force. Brownlie wrote in his book 'International Law and the Use of Force by States': 'The agency concerned cannot be confined to the military and other forces under the control of a ministry of defence or war, since the responsibility will be the same if a government acts through "militia", "security forces", or "police forces" which may be quite heavily armed and may employ armoured vehicles'.[94] He further clarified: 'Moreover, governments may act by means of completely "unofficial" agents, including armed bands, and "volunteers", or may give aid to groups of insurgents on the territory of another state'. Tams seems to agree with Brownlie.[95] In this book the term 'armed forces' is used to include not only regular armed forces but also security forces, police forces and irregular forces like militia and armed bands deployed by governments.

3.4.2 Coercive Intention

In the Cameroon v. Nigeria case, Nigeria claimed as follows:[96]

> 311. For its part, Nigeria states that it was not only in peaceful possession of the Lake Chad area and the Bakassi region at the time of the alleged invasions but had been since independence. Its deployment of force is alleged to have been for the purpose of resolving internal problems and responding to Cameroon's campaign of systematic encroachment on Nigerian territory. Nigeria claims to have acted in self-defence. It further contends that, even if the Court should find that Cameroon has sovereignty over these areas, the Nigerian presence there was the result of a "reasonable mistake" or "honest belief". Accordingly, Nigeria cannot be held internationally responsible for conduct which, at the time it took place, Nigeria had every reason to believe was lawful.

In this case, the ICJ decided:[97]

> … the Federal Republic of Nigeria is under an obligation expeditiously and without condition to withdraw its administration and its military and police forces from the territories which fall within the sovereignty of the Republic of Cameroon pursuant to points I and III of this operative paragraph.

But, as mentioned above, the ICJ also said:[98]

---

[94] Brownlie (1963), p. 361.

[95] Tams (2024), p. 312.

[96] The Cameroon v Nigeria judgment, para. 310.

[97] Ibid. para. 325. V.(A).

[98] Ibid. para. 319.

> 319. In the circumstances of the case, the Court considers moreover that, by the very fact of the present Judgment and of the evacuation of the Cameroonian territory occupied by Nigeria, the injury suffered by Cameroon by reason of the occupation of its territory will in all events have been sufficiently addressed. The Court will not therefore seek to ascertain whether and to what extent Nigeria's responsibility to Cameroon has been engaged as a result of that occupation.

Thus, the Court avoided the issue of violation of Article 2(4) of the UN Charter in this case.

Christine Gray wrote in her article on the Eritrea–Ethiopia Claims Commission (EECC): '[Nigeria's] use of force, if it had taken place in Cameroon's territory, was not an unlawful use of force but the result of reasonable mistake or honest belief. It had been in peaceful occupation of the Lake Chad region and of the Bakassi peninsula; it had used force only to resolve internal problems and in response to encroachment by Cameroon in self-defence. If it turned out that Cameroon was the lawful sovereign then Nigeria's use of force was reasonable mistake or honest belief.'[99]

Corten interpreted that the ICJ did not pronounce on the issue of violation of Article 2(4) in this case 'because of the not very serious character of the events in question'.[100] After examining the Temple of Preah Vihear case, where, according to Corten, the presence of three Thai guardians in Cambodian territory did not give rise to accusation based on PUF, but the dispatch of Thai troops did prompt Cambodia to accuse violation of Article 2(4), Corten concluded: 'Once again, everything will depend on the gravity of the act and the way it is seen to materialize one State's intention to use force against another. Should a genuine mistake occur where the State is not even aware of entering territory that is not under its sovereignty, the prohibition of the use of force will not, in principle, be involved'. Tams takes a similar position and writes: 'The approach of international courts and tribunals to date seems to imply that a State bona fide controlling a disputed border region lacks the required intent to coerce, so that its presence in the territory does not, in and of itself, amount to unlawful force, even if its territorial claim is eventually rejected'.

Corten and Tams seem to consider that coercive intention is required for the violation of Article 2(4). On the other hand, States may hide their intention and pretend to be without coercive intention. In the ICJ proceedings the party who had raised an issue has the burden of proof,[101] and, if a State deploys armed forces to an area known to be subject to competing claims, the State insisting on the absence of coercive intention seems to have the burden of proof to prove it.

In Case 1.0 in Sect. 3.3.3.4 above, where State A has peacefully established administration over the territory and maintained it without receiving protest from State B for 20 years, but after 20 years State B starts to protest to State A's administration and sends armed forces to the territory to deny the former State's administration and put it under its control, State B can be presumed to be attempting to coerce

[99] Gray (2006), p. 699.

[100] Corten (2010), p. 82.

[101] Riddell and Plant (2009), p. 89.

State A. Therefore, in this case, the deploying State must come up with convincing evidence to prove the absence of coercive intention.

If there is a specific area of land over which two States are making competing territorial claims which are known to each other but neither State has established administration over the area, and if one of them deploys armed forces to the area to take control, the deploying State is likely to have the intention to coerce the other claimant. In this case, the presumption against the absence of coercive intention is not as strong as in Case 1.0, but still the deploying State should provide evidence to prove the absence of coercive intention.

If there is a dispute between States over their border line but the exact location of the disputed area is not clear and no State has established administration over the area, as indicated in the Nigeria v Cameroon case, deployment of armed forces by a claimant State to the area might fall into the category of cases where the deploying State does not have intention to coerce another State. In this case, evidence required for the proof of the absence of coercive intention can be weaker than the above cases.

3.4.3 Non-Violent Use of Force

As will be discussed below, there have been cases where States succeeded in sending armed forces to a territory subject to competing claims, or even to another State's internationally recognised territory, without meeting resistance on the ground and, therefore, without firing weapons.[102] Once it succeeds in establishing a presence of armed forces, it can deter the other claimant from challenging the presence, as doing so is likely to lead to an armed conflict which may cause serious damage. Thus, even a non-violent use of armed force can change the *status quo* on the ground and create *fait accompli.*

In the Costa Rica v Nicaragua case, Nicaragua established military presence in the disputed territory, but in doing so it did not fire weapons. As mentioned above, in its judgment of 16 December 2015, the ICJ found that Costa Rica has sovereignty over the 'disputed territory'[103] and that Nicaragua has violated the territorial sovereignty of Costa Rica. Costa Rica asked the ICJ to find that Nicaragua breached PUF, and the ICJ said: 'The fact that Nicaragua considered that its activities were taking place on its own territory does not exclude the possibility of characterizing them as an unlawful use of force.'[104] However, it also found that 'by the very fact of the present Judgment and of the evacuation' of the disputed territory, the injury suffered by Costa Rica 'will in all events have been sufficiently addressed'.

In his separate opinion, Judge Owada argued: '... it is my view that it would have been more appropriate for the Court to have gone further by declaring that these

---

[102] Mikanagi (2018), pp. 1022–1025.

[103] The Costa Rica v Nicaragua judgment, p. 740, para. 229.

[104] Ibid. para. 97.

internationally wrongful acts by Nicaraguan authorities constituted an unlawful use of force under Article 2(4) of the United Nations Charter'.[105] Judge Robinson concurred with Judge Owada on this matter. In his separate opinion, quoting the reference to the Type II use of force in the 1970 Declaration, he pointed out: '... given that the location of the boundary was subject to a case before the Court, to the extent that Nicaragua's use of force may be seen "as a means of solving international disputes", it will violate the customary norm reflected in this duty'.[106] He also argued: 'The jurisprudence also establishes that non-violent use of force is not exempted from the prohibition. No shots need be fired, no heavy armaments need to be used and certainly no one need to be killed before a State can be said to have violated the prohibition.'[107]

In this case, Nicaragua's activities in the disputed territory did not involve any firing of weapons and it was described as a 'non-violent use of force' by Judge Robinson. In this book, the use of armed force that does not cause human injury or damage to property is called 'non-violent use of force'.[108]

The text of Article 2(4) does not clarify whether the term 'use' of force includes the deployment of armed forces that does not involve violent use of force. The ICJ's judgment did not address this question in the Costa Rica v Nicaragua judgment.[109]

Article 3(e) of the 'Definition of Aggression' annexed to GA resolution 3314 (XXIX) refers to 'the use of armed forces of one State which are within the territory of another State with the agreement of the receiving State, in contravention of the conditions provided for in the agreement or any extension of their presence in such territory beyond the termination of the agreement'.[110] This provision clearly shows that mere existence of armed forces without the consent of the receiving State may amount to aggression. Referring to this provision, Tams writes in his commentary on Article 2(4): 'as long as weapons are involved in an operation to deter or preempt resistance, they need not actually discharge; the unopposed invasion of foreign territory by a massively superior army is as much as a "use" of force as an armed force's unconsented "presence in [foreign] territory beyond the termination of the

[105] Separate Opinion of Judge Owada, Costa Rica v Nicaragua judgment, paras. 11–12.

[106] Separate Opinion of Judge Robinson, Costa Rica v Nicaragua judgment, para. 51.

[107] Ibid. para. 43.

[108] In the context of the law of international armed conflict, Dinstein defined 'violence' as acts that cause injury to human beings—either loss of life or other harm, whether physical or mental—or destruction of (or damage to) property. (Dinstein (2010), p. 1).

[109] In his Separate Opinion, Judge Robinson referred to the Corfu Channel judgment as relevant jurisprudence in his separate opinion in the Costa Rica v Nicaragua judgment, but while the ICJ found that the British naval activities in Albanian waters violated Albanian sovereignty, it did not directly pronounce upon whether there had been a violation of Article 2(4) of the UN Charter (Corfu Channel (United Kingdom v Albania), Merits, Judgment, 9 April 1949, ICJ Rep. (1949) p. 35).

[110] Ruys (2014), p. 189.

[stationing] agreement". In both instances, the *projection* of armed force is sufficient.'[111]

Another example of attempts to acquire territory by non-violent use of force would be Russia's attempt to annex Crimea in 2014. Crimea was internationally recognised territory of Ukraine in 2014. In March 2014, the so-called 'Little Green Men' were reported to be stealthily deployed to Crimea by Russia.,[112] and Russian armed forces stationed in Crimea also seemed to help the attempt. Russia called a referendum and signed a treaty for annexation and started to apply Russian law in Crimea. Neither Russian armed forces stationed in Crimea nor 'Little Green Men' opened fire or caused death, injury or destruction, but the annexation process seemed to have gone ahead with their help on the ground. The activities of the Russian armed force seemed to amount to 'the use of armed forces of one State which are within the territory of another State with the agreement of the receiving State, in contravention of the conditions provided for in the agreement or any extension of their presence in such territory beyond the termination of the agreement' mentioned in Article 3(e) of the 'Definition of Aggression'.

The UNGA resolution 68/262, adopted on 27 March 2014, which was voted on while Russia was still denying its involvement in the deployment of the irregular forces, indicates that the attempted annexation process of Crimea constituted unlawful acquisition of territory by force and therefore shall not be recognised. This resolution was adopted with 100 in favour, 11 against, 58 abstaining and 24 absent. It reads:[113]

> Recalling the obligations of all States under Article 2 of the Charter to refrain in their international relations from the threat or use of force against the territorial integrity or political independence of any State, and to settle their international disputes by peaceful means,
>
> Recalling also its resolution 2625 (XXV) of 24 October 1970, ... and reaffirming the principles contained therein that the territory of a State shall not be the object of acquisition by another State resulting from the threat or use of force, and that any attempt aimed at the partial or total disruption of the national unity and territorial integrity of a State or country or at its political independence is incompatible with the purposes and principles of the Charter,
>
> 1. Affirms its commitment to the sovereignty, political independence, unity and territorial integrity of Ukraine within its internationally recognized borders;
>
> 2. Calls upon all States to desist and refrain from actions aimed at the partial or total disruption of the national unity and territorial integrity of Ukraine, including any attempts to modify Ukraine's borders through the threat or use of force or other unlawful means; ...
>
> 6. Calls upon all States, international organizations and specialized agencies not to recognize any alteration of the status of the Autonomous Republic of Crimea and the city of Sevastopol on the basis of the above-mentioned referendum and to refrain from any action or dealing that might be interpreted as recognizing any such altered status.

Compared with GA resolutions ES-11/1 and ES-11/4 in 2022, the amount of support to this resolution was smaller. Nevertheless, 100 Member States which

---

[111] Tams (2024), p. 312.

[112] See Sect. 3.6.4 below.

[113] UN Doc. A/68/262.

supported this resolution seemed to confirm that the Russian attempt to acquire Crimea by force violated PATBF. The violation of PATBF must involve use of force under Article 2(4) of the UN Charter. Therefore, the non-violent use of armed force in the attempted annexation of Crimea in 2014 should be considered use of force under Article 2(4).

Considering the example of Crimea in 2014 and the reference to non-violent use of force in the 'Definition of Aggression', it seems reasonable to conclude that non-violent use of force may violate PUF and may also constitute the violation of PATBF.

3.4.4 Gravity of Use of Force

In his separate opinion on the Costa Rica v Nicaragua judgment, Judge Robinson referred to 'gravity' as a criterion for the use of force prohibited under Article 2(4) and considered the prolonged presence of military camps and personnel and the use of weapons such as anti-aircraft missiles as factors increasing the gravity.[114] The fact that the ICJ avoided finding on the violation of PUF in this case may indicate that Nicaragua's establishment of military presence in the Costa Rica v Nicaragua case was not grave enough to violate Article 2(4). Corten explained the ICJ's avoidance of pronouncement on the issue of Article 2(4) in the Cameroon v Nigeria judgment mainly on the basis of 'not very serious character'.[115]

Whether there is a threshold of gravity for violating PUF has been an issue discussed among scholars for some time. Corten argued that there is a threshold below which the use of force does not violate Article 2(4).[116] Ruys disagreed.[117] Tams writes that the 'better arguments suggest that a State only acts forcibly if, as a threshold matter, its conduct seeks to coerce the target'.[118]

Whether there is a threshold of gravity for violating PUF or not, higher gravity of use of force would contribute to the violation of PUF and PATBF. In the case of violent use of force, the gravity of use of force would mainly depend on the intensity of violence. In the case of non-violent use of force, the gravity of use of force would mainly depend on the potential destructive power of the weapons involved or the number of deployed personnel, and deployment of heavier weapons or larger number of personnel would be graver than deployment of smaller weapons or smaller number of personnel.

For example, in the Costa Rica v Nicaragua case, Costa Rica argued:[119]

---

[114] Separate opinion of Judge Robinson, the Costa Rica v Nicaragua judgment, paras. 43–53.

[115] Corten (2010), p. 82. In my ICLQ article, I also mentioned elements which relate to gravity, including the strength of the weapons deployed and the scale of the activities protected by the military presence (Mikanagi 2018, p. 1033).

[116] Corten (2010), pp. 55, 77.

[117] Ruys (2014), p. 159–160.

[118] Tams (2024), p. 315. See also Pobjie (2024), p. 158.

[119] ICJ CR 2011/1, p. 30.

> 24. On 31 October, Costa Rican police conducted another reconnaissance flight over Isla Portillos, and found that Costa Rica's flag had been removed, and that the Nicaraguan flag rose in its place. They also observed that several military camps had been established. The following day, on 1 November, a further fly-over determined the presence of armed Nicaraguan Army soldiers. You can see, from the projection that, as the aircraft carrying Costa Rican police passed, Nicaraguan soldiers pointed their weapons at it, in a sign of imminent confrontation: the photograph is at tab 63. One of the Nicaraguan Army personnel appears to be pointing an anti-aircraft type of weapon. Several other soldiers can be observed pointing their AK-47s at the aircraft as well. Given the potential for armed conflict – something that Costa Rica wished by all means to avoid – the Ministry of Public Security ceased all flights over in the area the following days.

In the 2005 Partial Award of the Eritrea–Ethiopia Claims Commission (EECC), the EECC found as follows:[120]

> 14. The evidence showed that, at about 5:30 a.m. on May 12, 1998, Eritrean armed forces, comprised of at least two brigades of regular soldiers, supported by tanks and artillery, attacked the town of Badme and several other border areas in Ethiopia's Tahtay Adiabo Wereda, as well as at least two places in its neighboring Laelay Adiabo Wereda. On that day and in the days immediately following, Eritrean armed forces then pushed across the flat Badme plain to higher ground in the east. Although the evidence regarding the nature of Ethiopian armed forces in the area conflicted, the weight of the evidence indicated that the Ethiopian defenders were composed merely of militia and some police, who were quickly forced to retreat by the invading Eritrean forces.

The anti-aircraft weapons held by soldiers mentioned by Costa Rica are probably weapons called man-portable air-defence systems (MANPADS or MPADS) which are usually categorised as small arms and light weapons (SALW).[121] Eritrea seemed to deploy heavier weapons than SALW, like tanks and artillery, and larger number of soldiers than Nicaragua. Military technology is developing rapidly, and there are also more modern defence systems consisting of radar and missiles covering the occupied area of land, which make it difficult for another State to enter the area without heavy damage and casualties.

3.4.5 Additional Elements Required for the Violation of PATBF

In the oral statement for the 2024 Advisory Opinion, Japan explained the basic concept of acquisition of territory by force as follows:[122]

> 5. Mr President, the acquisition of territory by force consists of two elements, namely (i) the establishment of control over the territory through forcible measures and (ii) the intention

[120] The 2005 EECC Partial Award, p. 465, para. 14.

[121] 'International Instrument to Enable States to Identify and Trace, in a Timely and Reliable Manner, Illicit Small Arms and Light Weapons' adopted by UNGA in 2005 provides definitions for small armed and light weapons (UN Doc. A/60/88).

[122] ICJ CR 2024/9, p. 49, para. 5.

> to appropriate that territory permanently. ... By "acquisition" or indeed "annexation" of territory by force, we mean a situation where a State attempts to acquire territorial title on the basis of forcible acts and where the State does not otherwise have valid title to that territory.

These elements were based on the definition of annexation in the Max Planck Encyclopaedia of Public International Law.[123] In the Advisory Opinion issued on 19 July 2024, the ICJ said:[124]

> 158. By the term "annexation", in the present context, the Court understands the forcible acquisition by the occupying Power of the territory that it occupies, namely its integration into the territory of the occupying Power. Annexation, then, presupposes the intent of the occupying Power to exercise permanent control over the occupied territory.

According to the Separate Opinion of Judge Cleveland:[125]

> 29. While many participants in these proceedings contended that at least part of the Occupied Palestinian Territory has been annexed, few addressed the meaning of this concept. Japan, however, elaborated on the forcible acquisition of territory in its submissions, stating that the principle consists of "the establishment of control over the territory through forcible measures", coupled with "the intention to appropriate that territory permanently". ...
> 30. The Court's predominant reasoning is consistent with this approach. The Court makes clear that the essence of the prohibition of the acquisition of territory by force involves the use of force to control a foreign territory, with the intent of exercising permanent control. Thus, the Court observes that annexation "presupposes the intent of the occupying Power to exercise permanent control over the occupied territory" (Advisory Opinion, para. 158; see also paragraphs 159 and 161).

The violation of PATBF requires (i) acts involving use of armed force under Article 2(4) of the UN Charter which establish control over the territory, (ii) with the intent of exercising permanent control over the territory.

3.4.5.1 Establishment of Control through Coercive Measures

As mentioned above, Tams considers coercion to be an element constituting unlawful use of force, and writes: 'For Article 2(4) to apply, it is necessary that a State 'wants to force the other State ... to do or to refrain from doing something."[126] Regarding the coercive effect of acts constituting violation of PATBF, the ICJ said in paragraph 121 of the 2004 Wall Advisory Opinion:[127]

> The Court considers that the construction of the wall and its associated regime create a "fait accompli" on the ground that could well become permanent, in which case, and notwith-

[123] Hofmann (2020), p. 408.

[124] The 2024 ICJ Advisory Opinion, para. 159.

[125] Separate Opinion of Judge Cleveland, the 2024 ICJ Advisory Opinion, paras. 29–30.

[126] Tams (2024), pp. 315–316. Corten (2010), p. 76.

[127] The 2004 ICJ Wall Advisory Opinion, para. 121.

standing the formal characterization of the wall by Israel, it would be tantamount to de facto annexation.

The construction of the wall by Israel in the OPT did not itself involve actual use of weapons, but Israel's measures in the OPT have been taken as a part of its occupation since 1967 and it has been accompanied by the creation of a new administrative regime through the order of the Israeli Defence Forces (IDF).[128] In this Advisory Opinion, the Court did not make clear determination on PATBF, but paragraph121 seems to indicate that the effect of creating *fait accompli* tantamount to de facto annexation could make the construction of the wall and its associated regime amount to violation of PATBF. The construction of the wall and its associated regime created *fait accompli* through their coercive effect. The establishment of control through coercive measures involving armed forces is a necessary element for the acquisition of territory by force, and it can be achieved through deployment of armed forces and following measures backed by the armed force which create *fait accompli* by making it materially impossible for another claimant to restore the *status quo ante* in the territory without risking human injury or damage to property.[129]

3.4.5.2 Acts Displaying Intent to Exercise Permanent Control

3.4.5.2.1 Explicit Measures to Annex Territory

As mentioned above, a State attempting to acquire territory by force typically deploys armed forces to an area of land which is not within its internationally recognised border nor under its existing administration, puts it under its control, and takes explicit measures to annex it to its territory, which expresses intent to exercise permanent control over the territory. Such explicit measures to annex the territory may take various forms, including an official declaration of such an intention, legislation to put the area of land in the territory and publication of an official map showing the area as its territory. In the case of Russia's attempt to acquire Crimea in 2014, Russia signed a treaty for annexation and extended the application of Russia's law to Crimea. As also mentioned above, some of these measures might be taken before the deployment. In such cases, these measures do not take effect on the ground before the deployment but start to take effect on the ground after the establishment of control over the territory.

[128] Ibid. para. 85.

[129] Mikanagi (2018), pp. 1032–1033.

3.4.5.2.2 Conduct Establishing Permanent Control

In the case of Israel's policies and practice in the OPT examined in the 2024 ICJ Advisory Opinion, Israel did not formally express its intention to annex the OPT. Therefore, the Court found that conduct displaying intent of the occupying Power to exercise permanent control over the occupied territory is required, and it examined what kind of conduct displays such an intent. The measures found by the ICJ in this Opinion to display the intent to exercise permanent control are, therefore, not required for the violation of acquisition of territory by force through deployment of armed forces accompanied by explicit measures to annex the territory, which are mentioned above.

In the 2024 Advisory Opinion, the Court found that 'policies and practices designed to remain in place indefinitely and to create irreversible effects on the ground'[130] establish 'permanent control over the territory'[131] and amount to the violation of PATBF.[132]

As quoted above, Judge Cleveland explained that the ICJ's predominant reasoning is consistent with Japan's approach. Japan called an attempt to acquire territory without formal expression of intention to annex it '*de facto* annexation', and explained it as follows:[133]

> 6. The clearest case of annexation is an attempt to annex occupied territory *de jure*. In such a circumstance, the occupying State formally declares its sovereignty over the annexed territory.
> 7. However, in the *Wall* Advisory Opinion, this Court indicated that annexation could also take place *de facto* where the actions of a State lead to what the Court called a "fait accompli", that is, a situation on the ground which becomes permanent and which others are compelled to accept. A State seeking to avoid the denunciation of the international community may be incentivized to refrain from formally declaring the annexation of territory. Without clearly expressing its intention to annex the territory, it may seek to gain permanent control over a territory it occupies by engaging in military operations and taking a series of measures that make it materially impossible for other claimants to restore the *status quo ante* without risking death, physical injury or damage to property. In other words, the occupying State may create what you called a "fait accompli" through these measures.

This explanation was based on the contents of paragraph 121 of the 2004 Wall Advisory Opinion. Japan further argued that acts which have continuous coercive effect in imposing control over territory may create a *fait accompli* and are likely to indicate intention to annex the territory. The 2024 ICJ Advisory Opinion uses an expression similar to this statement and argues that conduct by the occupying Power that displays 'an intent to exercise permanent control over the occupied territory may indicate an act of annexation'. Paragraph 159 of the Opinion reads as follows:[134]

---

[130] The 2024 ICJ Advisory Opinion, para. 172.

[131] The 2024 ICJ Advisory Opinion, para. 161.

[132] The 2024 ICJ Advisory Opinion, para. 179.

[133] ICJ CR 2024/9, p. 49, paras. 6 and 7.

[134] The 2024 ICJ Advisory Opinion, paras. 159–160.

> 159. The Court recalls, in this regard, that, under the law of occupation, the control of the occupied territory by the occupying Power must be temporary in character. ... Consequently, conduct by the occupying Power that displays an intent to exercise permanent control over the occupied territory may indicate an act of annexation.

Paragraph 160 of the Opinion also reads as follows:

> 160. The assertion by the occupying Power of permanent control of the occupied territory may manifest itself in a variety of ways. In this connection, the Court notes that a distinction between "*de jure*" and "*de facto*" annexation is occasionally made, including by some of the participants in these proceedings. According to this distinction, *de jure* annexation consists in the formal declaration by the occupying Power of sovereignty over the occupied territory, whereas *de facto* annexation comprises acts short of a formal declaration that create a "fait accompli" on the ground and that consolidate the occupying Power's permanent control over the occupied territory. Although differing in terms of the means through which the annexation is carried out, both types of annexation share the same objective — the assertion of permanent control over the occupied territory.

Thus, the Court does not use the term '*de facto* annexation' and it takes the position that conduct displaying intent to exercise permanent control over the OPT indicates an act of annexation. Based on this position, the Court examines 'whether through its conduct, Israel establishes its permanent control over the Occupied Palestine Territory, in a manner that would amount to annexation'.[135]

Japan further elaborated on examples of acts which indicate intention to permanently exercise sovereignty over the territory, and in so doing Japan emphasised the importance of continuous and irreversible effects of these acts on the territory. The relevant part of the oral statement is as follows:[136]

> 10. ... The following acts by occupying States may have such continuous coercive effects:
>
> – *First*, large-scale alteration of the demographic composition of the territory, backed by military and other physical power, including through expropriation of land and eviction of the population.
>
> – *Second*, the construction and continued maintenance by an occupying Power of a network of physical infrastructure, particularly where these represent such significant financial investment that they may be deemed to be intended to subsist over a significant period of time. This may include, for example, roads, communication systems, healthcare facilities or large-scale military or law enforcement facilities.
>
> – *Third*, the continuous forcible seizure and exploitation of the natural resources, including water, by an occupying Power.
>
> 11. These acts do not necessarily cause death, injury or destruction, but when they are implemented cumulatively at a significant scale and sustained for a long period, they would have continuous, even irreversible, effect on the territory. In such a case there may be evidence that the occupying State's intention is to permanently establish sovereignty over the relevant area, even if it is doing so incrementally. If such acts are accompanied by statements of State officials affirming the irreversibility of measures or even asserting the intent to establish sovereignty over the occupied territories, the measures I have just mentioned above are even more likely to indicate intention to acquire territory and thus amount to a prohibited attempt to acquire territory by force.

---

[135] The 2024 ICJ Advisory Opinion, para. 161.

[136] ICJ CR 2024/9, p. 50, paras. 10–11.

The ICJ mentioned elements similar to those mentioned in the Japanese statement. The Court emphasised the importance of 'policies and practices designed to remain in place indefinitely and to create irreversible effects on the ground'. Paragraphs 170 and 173 of the Opinion read:[137]

> 170. Israel's extension of its domestic law to the West Bank, notably to the settlements and over the settlers (see paragraphs 134–141 above), as well as its assumption of broader regulatory powers by virtue of the prolonged character of the occupation, entrenches its control over the occupied territory. Israel has also taken steps to incorporate the West Bank into its own territory. In this regard, the Court takes note of Israel's transfer of powers, including land designations, planning and co-ordination of demolitions, to a civilian administration within the Ministry of Defence in 2023 (see also paragraph 156 above). This is in line with the Israeli Government's guiding principles of 2022, which announced the formulation and promotion of a policy for the "application of sovereignty" over the West Bank ("A coalition agreement to establish a national government" (28 December 2022), para. 118). ...
> 173. In light of the above, the Court is of the view that Israel's policies and practices, including the maintenance and expansion of settlements, the construction of associated infrastructure, including the wall, the exploitation of natural resources, the proclamation of Jerusalem as Israel's capital, the comprehensive application of Israeli domestic law in East Jerusalem and its extensive application in the West Bank, entrench Israel's control of the Occupied Palestinian Territory, notably of East Jerusalem and of Area C of the West Bank. These policies and practices are designed to remain in place indefinitely and to create irreversible effects on the ground. Consequently, the Court considers that these policies and practices amount to annexation of large parts of the Occupied Palestinian Territory. ...

In the paragraphs above, the Court also mentioned 'a coalition agreement', and Japan also mentioned a statement from government officials in the paragraph quoted above. They do not seem to be treated by the ICJ as formal expressions of intention to annex but they are treated as a part of policies and practices designed to remain in place indefinitely and to create irreversible effects on the ground. So, for the Court, 'policies and practice designed to remain in place indefinitely and to create irreversible effects on the ground' establish permanent control over the territory and amount to annexation. Thus, in the 2024 ICJ Advisory Opinion, the lack of formal expression of intention to exercise sovereignty seems to be supplemented by 'policies and practices entrenching control and designed to remain in place indefinitely and to create irreversible effects on the ground'.

On the other hand, as mentioned above, in the case of Russia's attempt to annex Crimea in 2014, the presence of Russian armed forces followed by a referendum, treaty for annexation and application of Russian law in Crimea was considered by 100 Member States which supported GA resolution 68/262 as sufficient to violate PATBF. These measures did not have irreversible effects on the ground, and when the deploying State expresses its intention to exercise sovereignty, the creation of irreversible effects on the ground would not be required for the violation of PATBF.

[137] The 2024 ICJ Advisory Opinion, paras. 170, 173.

3.5 Hypothetical Scenarios with Combinations of Elements

In the following, three hypothetical scenarios of possible attempts to acquire territory by force which consist of different contexts and acts will be examined. These scenarios will be examined in comparison with the cases discussed in this chapter, including the Russian attempt to annex Crimea in 2014, the Costa Rica v Nicaragua case, the Eritrea–Ethiopia case, and possible cases exceeding thresholds for the violation of PUF and PATBF will be explored. In each scenario, actions to be taken by third States and UN organs will also be suggested.

Third States have an obligation not to recognise the unlawful acquisition of territory by force, and this obligation comes with the responsibility for third States to be vigilant about possible cases of attempts to acquire territory by force and be ready to apply PATBF to such cases.

The following scenarios are based on contextual elements and acts involving use of force examined above. They are neither comprehensive nor conclusive but intend to provide food for thought for thinking about possible combinations of various elements amounting to the violation of PUF and PATBF.

Scenario 1: Internationally Recognised Territory
Scenario 1–1: Non-Violent Deployment

State B stealthily or discreetly deploys armed forces to an area of land within State A's internationally recognised territory without firing weapons and installs a modern defence system of radar and missiles in the area.

Scenario 1–2: Violent Deployment

State B deploys armed forces to an area of land within State A's internationally recognised territory. The deployment meets the resistance of State A's patrolling police or armed forces, but, by firing weapons at the patrolling police or armed forces, State B's armed forces succeed in occupying the area.

Scenario 1–3: Measures to Annex

After Scenarios 1–1 and 1–2, State B declares the annexation of the area and starts to apply its law.

State B's deployment of armed forces violates State A's existing internationally recognised territory and it seems to fit the description of the violation of the prohibition of the Type II use of force in the 1970 Declaration.

As quoted above, Article 3(a) of 'Definition of Aggression' provides: 'The invasion or attack by the armed forces of a State of the territory of another State, or any military occupation, however temporary, resulting from such invasion or attack, or any annexation by the use of force of the territory of another State or part thereof'. The term 'attack' here seems to indicate use of force involving firing of weapons but, if there is no active resistance on the ground, the 'invasion' can succeed without firing weapons. The terms 'invasion' and 'attack' seem to exclude cases of honest mistake. If a State deploys armed forces to the area of another State's internationally recognised territory and takes control of the territory, it amounts to the invasion and occupation mentioned in this Article 3(a) and it is likely to violate PUF unless justified by the right to self-defence.

As mentioned above, Article 3(e) of the 'Definition of Aggression' also refers to 'the use of armed forces of one State which are within the territory of another State with the agreement of the receiving State, in contravention of the conditions provided for in the agreement or any extension of their presence in such territory beyond the termination of the agreement'.[138] If the armed forces are deployed to another State's internationally recognised territory without the latter State's consent, regardless of the absence of violent use of force, this Article 3(e) will apply and the deployment will violate PUF unless it is due to an honest mistake.

Therefore, State B's deployment to the area of land in State A's internationally recognised territory to take control over it in Scenarios 1–1 and 1–2 amounts to a violation of PUF.

In Scenario 1–3, as State B is expressing intention to exercise sovereignty and implementing measures to annex the territory, like Russia did in Crimea in 2014, it should amount to a violation of PATBF.

Actions Against State B

Scenarios 1–1 and 1–2

As they are clear cases of violation of PUF, third States should not support State B's deployment of armed forces and immediately call on State B to stop the deployment.

The Security Council should also immediately call on State B to stop the deployment of armed forces. If the Council cannot act due to veto, the GA can also call on State B to stop the deployment of armed forces.

Scenario 1–3

When State B declares an annexation, third States must refrain from recognising the area as State B's territory and should call on State B to stop the attempt to acquire territory by force. Obligations for third States arising from the violation of PATBF will be examined in Sect. 4.2 below.

The Security Council should also call on State B to stop the attempt to acquire territory by force and call on third States not to recognise the area as State B's territory. If the Council cannot act due to veto, the GA can also call on State B to stop the attempt to acquire territory by force and call on third States not to recognise the area as State B's territory.

In this scenario third States might be put under various political pressures not to make their positions clear on this kind of situation. The voting record on draft GA resolutions on 24 February 2025 clearly shows this political difficulty in saying the right thing.

GA resolution ES-11/7 adopted on 24 February 2025 was an updated version of GA resolution ES-11/1 marking 3 years since the invasion of Ukraine started. The amount of support it managed to secure decreased from 141 for GA resolution

[138] Ruys (2014), p. 189.

ES-11/1 to 93 for GA resolution ES-11/7. There were only 7 Member States which moved from support to against, but 33 moved from support to abstention, and 8 moved from support to not voting. The number of Member States voting against increased from 5 to 18, the number of those abstaining increased from 35 to 65 and those who did not vote increased from 12 to 17.

Records of votes by Member States on these resolutions can be easily found on the UN website. What States do in the critical juncture of history will be reviewed in the future and remembered. As was briefly explained in Chap. 2, Japan stood on the wrong side of the history of international efforts towards strengthening rule of law against attempts to acquire territory by force in the 1930s. Positions taken by States in the GA matter a lot as subsequent practice under Article 31(3) of the VCLT or as evidence for the identification of customary international law. Therefore, States should bear in mind that their votes will be remembered and have an impact in the course of international law.

Scenario 2: Peacefully Established Administration for 20 Years

State A has been openly and constantly taking administrative measures regulating the activities of people in an area of land for 20 years. State B has not been in a national emergency or other conditions which hinders it to take measures relating to the territory, but it has not protested to State A's administration. State A has deposited declaration under Article 36(2) of the ICJ Statute accepting the ICJ's jurisdiction over issues relating to territory and use of force, but State B has not deposited declaration under Article 36(2) of the ICJ Statute. After 20 years of peacefully established administration by State A, State B starts to claim its sovereignty over the area. There is no treaty between State A and State B clearly referring to the area as State B's territory, and during the 20 years State A did not notice State B's administrative measures regulating activities in the area.

Scenario 2–1: Non-Violent Deployment

State B stealthily or discreetly deploys armed forces to the area and puts it under control without firing weapons and installs a modern defence system of radar and missiles. State B declares the annexation of the area and starts to apply its law.

Scenario 2–2: Violent Deployment

State B deploys armed forces to the area. The deployment of armed forces meets the resistance of State A's patrolling police, but, by firing weapons at the patrolling police, State B's armed forces succeed in occupying the area. State B declares the annexation of the area and starts to apply its law.

Costa Rica was found by the ICJ to have sovereignty over the territory in question, and Costa Rica's territorial title, if known, should have been protected by PUF and PATBF. However, Costa Rica's territorial title based on an earlier treaty and relevant awards was disputed by Nicaragua and Costa Rica did not establish administration over the disputed territory. In Scenario 2, State A has peacefully established administration for 20 years, and this peacefully established administration deserves protection by the prohibition of Type II use of force.

Furthermore, compared with the Costa Rica v Nicaragua case, the following elements strengthen elements contributing to the violation of PUF:

- State B resorting to armed forces as a means of settlement despite State A's acceptance of ICJ's jurisdiction.
- State B's deployment of a modern defence system of radar and missiles (2–1);
- State B's firing of weapons at State A's policing force (2–2).

Therefore, in both Scenarios 2–1 and 2–2, State B's deployment of armed forces is likelier to violate PUF than Nicaragua's deployment of armed forces in the Costa Rica v Nicaragua case.

Compared with the Eritrea–Ethiopia case, as State A's administration has been peacefully established for 20 years, it deserves stronger protection against the Type II use of force than Ethiopia's *de facto* 'peaceful administration'. State B's violent deployment of armed forces in Scenario 2–2 is likelier or at least equally likely to violate PUF compared with Eritrea's deployment of armed forces to Badme. The non-violent deployment in Scenario 2–1 may be weaker in its intensity of violence than Eritrea's attack on Badme in 1998, but the peacefully established administration for 20 years seems likely to compensate for this weakness to some extent and seems fairly likely to violate PUF.

If there is also evidence showing that State B has become aware of State A's administration but did not protest as in Case 1.1 in Sect. 3.3.3.4, the State A's administration would deserve even stronger protection against the Type II use of force and State B's deployment of armed forces would become likelier to violate PUF.

Actions Against State B
Scenarios 2–1 and 2–2

Third States should call on State B to stop the deployment. The Security Council should call on State B to stop the deployment of armed forces. If the Council cannot act due to veto, the GA should call on State B to stop the deployment of armed forces.

As pointed out above, it is difficult to determine whether 20 years of peacefully established administration creates a valid territorial title, and it requires case-by-case analysis. However, if there is evidence showing that State B has become aware of State A's administration but did not protest, as in Case 1.1 in Sect. 3.3.3.4, it would strengthen State A's position against State B and make it difficult for State B to argue that it honestly believed that it had a stronger territorial title than State A. In such a case, as in Case 1.1, there would be at least a possibility of State B's violation of PATBF, and, in view of avoiding the violation of the obligations for a third State arising from possible violation of PATBF, third States should look for evidence indicating State B's awareness of State A's administrative measures. If there is such evidence, they should precautionarily refrain from recognising the territory in question as State B's territory as much as possible, since there is no legal obligation to do so.

Scenario 3: Peacefully Established Administration for 50 Years

State A has been openly and constantly taking administrative measures regulating the activities of people in an area of land for 50 years. State B has not been in a national emergency or other conditions which hinders it from taking measures relating to the area, but it has not protested about State A's administration for 50 years. State A has deposited a declaration under Article 36(2) of the ICJ Statute accepting the ICJ's jurisdiction over issues relating to territory and use of force, but State B has not deposited a declaration under Article 36(2) of the ICJ Statute. After 50 years of peacefully established administration by State A, State B starts to claim its sovereignty over the area. There is no treaty between State A and State B clearly referring to the area as State B's territory.

Scenario 3–1: Non-Violent Deployment

State B stealthily or discreetly deploys armed forces to the area and puts it under control without firing weapons and installs a modern defence system of radar and missiles. State B declares the annexation of the area and starts to apply its law.

Scenario 3–2: Violent Deployment

State B deploys armed forces to the area. The deployment of armed forces meets the resistance of State A's patrolling police, but, by firing weapons at the patrolling police, State B's armed forces succeed in occupying the area. State B declares the annexation of the area and starts to apply its law.

State A's peacefully established administration for 50 years deserves even stronger protection against the Type II use of force than the peacefully established administration for 20 years in Scenario 3. Therefore, both the violent deployment in Scenario 3–2 and non-violent deployment in Scenario 3–1 are even likelier to violate the prohibition of the Type II use of force than in Scenarios 2–1 and 2–2.

Actions Against State B

Scenarios 3–1 and 3–2

As in Scenarios 2-1 and 2-2, third States should call on State B to stop the deployment. The Security Council should call on State B to stop the deployment of armed forces. If the Council cannot act due to veto, the GA should call on State B to stop the deployment of armed forces.

Peacefully established administration for 50 years without State B's protest, while case-by-case analysis is necessary, strongly indicates State A's consolidation of territorial title, and makes it difficult to believe that State B honestly believed that it had a stronger territorial title based on international law than State A. Therefore, there is a possibility that, through the establishment of control and measures to annex the territory, State B has also violated PATBF. Third States should take this possibility fully into account in responding to the situation. In view of avoiding the violation of the obligations for the third State, which will be examined below, third States should at least precautionarily refrain from recognising the territory in question as State B's territory, since there is no legal obligation to do so. If after 50 years' silence State B starts to claim that it has strong evidence of territorial title, the third State should look at the evidence with caution. As long as third States are not convinced that the evidence presented by State B outweighs State A's peaceful administration over 50 years, they should refrain from recognising State B's sovereignty over the territory.

In Scenarios 2 and 3, the ICJ does not have jurisdiction due to State B's unwillingness, and third States cannot expect third-party dispute settlement between State A and State B. If there is ambiguity about the legal situation, the Security Council can make recommendations under Article 36 of the UN Charter to bring the case before the ICJ.

Article 36 provides that:

1. The Security Council may, at any stage of a dispute of the nature referred to in Article 33 or of a situation of like nature, recommend appropriate procedures or methods of adjustment.
2. The Security Council should take into consideration any procedures for the settlement of the dispute which have already been adopted by the parties.
3. In making recommendations under this Article the Security Council should also take into consideration that legal disputes should as a general rule be referred by the parties to the International Court of Justice in accordance with the provisions of the Statute of the Court.

This provision has rarely been utilised, but in the Corfu Channel case, on 9 April 1947, the Council adopted the following resolution

> The Security Council having considered statements of representatives of the United Kingdom and Albania concerning a dispute between the United Kingdom and Albania arising out of an incident on 22nd October, 1946, in the Strait of Corfu in which two British ships were damaged by mines with resulting loss of life and injury to their crews recommends that the United Kingdom and Albanian Governments should immediately refer the dispute to the International Court of Justice in accordance with the provisions of the Statute of the Court.

If State B is a permanent member of the Security Council, Article 27(3) of the UN Charter should apply. Article 27(3) provides that:

> Decisions of the Security Council on all other matters shall be made by an affirmative vote of nine members including the concurring votes of the permanent members; provided that, in decisions under Chapter VI, and under paragraph 3 of Article 52, a party to a dispute shall abstain from voting.

In Scenarios 1–3 above, especially in scenarios likelier to amount to the violation of PATBF, if the Security Council cannot act due to veto, the GA's role would become crucial, as we have seen in the situations relating to Ukraine and Gaza. For example, as mentioned above, GA resolution 77/126 of 12 December 2022 seemed to play a crucial role in convincing the ICJ judges to apply PATBF to the OPT in the 2024 ICJ Advisory Opinion.

Looking back to a century ago, the League of Nations could adopt a resolution against Japan finding violation of Article 2 of the 1928 Kellogg-Briand Pact. Article 2 of the Pact, which has contents similar to Article 2(3) of the UN Charter, provides:

> The High Contracting Parties agree that the settlement or solution of all disputes or conflicts of whatever nature or of whatever origin they may be, which may arise among them, shall never be sought except by pacific means.

The report of the Assembly of the League of Nations adopted on 24 February 1933, 89 years earlier from the Russian invasion of Ukraine in 2022, reads:[139]

> The Assembly, in view of the failure of the efforts which, under Article 15, paragraph 3, of the Covenant, it was its duty to make with a view to effecting a settlement of the dispute submitted for its consideration under paragraph 9 of the said article, adopts, in virtue of paragraph 4 of that article, the following report containing a statement of the facts of the dispute and the recommendations which are deemed just and proper in regard thereto.
>
> ...
>
> Part IV Statement of the Recommendations ...
>
> Section II
>
> The provisions of this section constitute the recommendations of the Assembly under Article 15, paragraph 4, of the Covenant.
>
> Having defined the principles, conditions and considerations applicable to the settlement of the dispute,
>
> The Assembly recommends as follows:
>
> 1. Whereas the sovereignty over Manchuria belongs to China,
>
> A. Considering that the presence of Japanese troops outside the zone of the South Manchuria Railway and their operations outside this zone are incompatible with the legal principles which should govern the settlement of the dispute, and that it is necessary to establish as soon as possible a situation consistent with these principles. ...

The League of Nations could at least find that what Japan was doing was against the principle of peaceful settlement of dispute. The United Nations should be able to do better.[140]

If a GA resolution condemning the deployment of armed forces as violation of PUF is adopted with overwhelming support such as 140 with a small number of States against being less than 10, it should have a significant weight in indicating the violation of PUF. If a GA resolution condemning State B's violation of PATBF and calling on Member States not to recognise State B's sovereignty over the territory is adopted by a similar majority, it should also have a significant weight in indicating violation of PATBF.

3.6 The Issue of Attribution to a State

3.6.1 Crimea in 2014

As mentioned above, in March 2014, the so-called 'Little Green Men' were reported to be stealthily deployed to Crimea by Russia, and the annexation process seemed to have proceeded with their help on the ground.[141] If the deployment of 'Little

[139] Report Provided for in Article 15, Paragraph 4, of the Covenant, Adopted by the Special Assembly of the League of Nations, 24 February 1933, in Hudson (1933a) (Verdict of the League), p. 78.

[140] See also Hudson (1933b) (AJIL), pp. 303–304.

[141] O'Connell (2018), pp. 855–866.

Green Men' was attributable to Russia, it would have amounted to the violation of PUF through deployment of irregular forces to another State's internationally recognised territory without the latter State's consent. Support by 100 Member States to GA resolution 68/262 was weaker than the support to GA resolutions on the Russian invasion of Ukraine in 2022 such as ES-11/1 on the aggression itself and ES-11/4 on the attempt to annex Ukrainian territory. The difficulty in the attribution of the deployment of those irregular forces to Russia might have worked negatively for third States in determining whether this situation amounted to the violation of PUF and PATBF.

3.6.2 *Rules on Attribution*[142]

Article 2 of the ILC's Articles on State Responsibility clarifies the two elements constituting internationally wrongful acts: 'There is an internationally wrongful act of a State when conduct consisting of an action or omission: (a) is attributable to the State under international law; and (b) constitutes a breach of an international obligation of the State'.[143]

Article 8 of the ILC's Articles on State Responsibility provides:[144]

> The conduct of a person or group of persons shall be considered an act of a State under international law if the person or group of persons is in fact acting on the instructions of, or under the direction or control of, that State in carrying out the conduct.

Article 8 refers to instruction, direction, or control. These terms are not clearly defined, but the article seems to require specificity concerning the State's influence over the conduct in question. In the 2007 Bosnian Genocide judgment, the ICJ said, after quoting the Nicaragua judgment, 'It must however be shown that this 'effective control' was exercised, or that the State's instructions were given, in respect of each operation in which the alleged violations occurred, not generally in respect of the overall actions taken by the persons or groups of persons having committed the violations'.[145]

In rejecting the International Criminal Tribunal for the former Yugoslavia's Appeals Chamber's application of the 'overall control' test, the ICJ said:[146]

---

[142] See Mikanagi and Mačák (2020) pp. 60–68. Mikanagi (2021) p. 1019.

[143] Report of the International Law Commission on the work of its fifty-third session, 23 April–1 June and 2 July–10 August 2001, Official Records of the General Assembly, Fifty-sixth session, Supplement No.10, UN Doc. A/56/10 [hereinafter cited as UN Doc. A/56/10].

[144] Ibid.

[145] Application of the Convention on the Prevention and Punishment of the Crime of Genocide (Bosn. & Herz. v. Serb. & Montenegro), Judgment, ICJ Rep. (2007) [hereinafter cited as the Bosnia Genocide judgment], p. 208 para. 400.

[146] Ibid. p. 210, para. 406.

> [A] State's responsibility can be incurred for acts committed by persons or groups of persons—neither State organs nor to be equated with such organs—only if, assuming those acts to be internationally wrongful, they are attributable to it under the rule of customary international law reflected in Article 8 … This is so where an organ of the State gave the instructions or provided the direction pursuant to which the perpetrators of the wrongful act acted or where it exercised effective control over the action during which the wrong was committed.

The ILC's commentary on Article 8 of the Articles on State Responsibility also made clear that the instructions, direction, or control must relate to the conduct that is said to have amounted to an internationally wrongful act.[147]

While the Articles on State Responsibility clarify the rules concerning attribution to States, it does not deal with the issue of proof,[148] and it is not clear to what extent the attribution must be proven. With regard to acceptable evidence for the proof of attribution, the 1949 Corfu Channel judgment said that, when the victim State is unable to present direct proof due to the exclusive territorial control by the respondent, such a State 'should be allowed a more liberal recourse to inferences of fact and circumstantial evidence,'[149] and that indirect and circumstantial evidence is to be accorded 'special weight' when it is based on a series of facts which are linked together and lead logically to a single conclusion.[150] In addition, this judgment indicated the relationship between the gravity of charges and the standard of proof.[151] In her separate opinion in the 2003 Oil Platforms judgment, Judge Higgins referred to a general agreement that graver charges require a higher standard of proof.[152]

The bar set by the ICJ for the proof of attribution to a State based on effective control tends to be rather high. For example, in the Oil Platforms case, the discovery of moored mines bearing serial numbers matching other Iranian mines in the same area as the mine attack on the U.S. warship USS Samuel B. Roberts—in particular those found aboard an Iranian vessel boarded by U.S. forces—did not convince the ICJ that USS Samuel B. Roberts struck a mine laid by Iran.[153] This evidence indicated a strong relationship between the mines laid in the area of the incident and Iran. However, the ICJ noted that Iraq was also laying mines during the Iran–Iraq War, and the evidence shown by the United States could not logically exclude alternative interpretations not leading to Iran.[154]

---

147 UN Doc. A/56/10, p. 48.

148 Ibid. p. 54, 72.

149 Corfu Channel (United Kingdom v Albania), Merits, Judgment, 9 April 1949, ICJ Rep. (1949) p. 18.

150 Ibid. p. 18.

151 Ibid. p. 17.

152 Case Concerning Oil Platforms (Islamic Republic of Iran v USA), Judgment, 6 November 2003, ICJ Rep. (2003) [hereinafter cited as the Oil Platform judgment] Separate Opinion of Judge Higgins, p.234, para.33. See also Mikanagi and Mačák (2020), pp. 65–66.

153 The Oil Platform judgment, pp. 194–195, paras. 70–71.

154 Mikanagi (2021), p. 1029.

States may have evidence for attribution in accordance with Article 8 of the ILC Articles on State Responsibility meeting the standards of proof required by the ICJ. On the other hand, when such evidence for proving attribution in accordance with Article 8 is not available, Article 11 of the ILC Articles on State Responsibility may prove useful. Article 11 provides that:[155]

> **Article 11** Conduct acknowledged and adopted by a State as its own Conduct which is not attributable to a State under the preceding articles shall nevertheless be considered an act of that State under international law if and to the extent that the State acknowledges and adopts the conduct in question as its own.

The commentary on this article explains this acknowledgment and adoption of the conduct in question 'as its own' as follows:[156]

> (6) The phrase "acknowledges and adopts the conduct in question as its own" is intended to distinguish cases of acknowledgement and adoption from cases of mere support or endorsement. ICJ in the United States Diplomatic and Consular Staff in Tehran case used phrases such as "approval", "endorsement", "the seal of official governmental approval" and "the decision to perpetuate [the situation]". These were sufficient in the context of that case, but as a general matter, conduct will not be attributable to a State under article 11 where a State merely acknowledges the factual existence of conduct or expresses its verbal approval of it. In international controversies, States often take positions which amount to "approval" or "endorsement" of conduct in some general sense but do not involve any assumption of responsibility. The language of "adoption", on the other hand, carries with it the idea that the conduct is acknowledged by the State as, in effect, its own conduct. Indeed, provided the State's intention to accept responsibility for otherwise non-attributable conduct is clearly indicated, article 11 may cover cases where a State has accepted responsibility for conduct of which it did not approve, which it had sought to prevent and which it deeply regretted. However such acceptance may be phrased in the particular case, the term "acknowledges and adopts" in article 11 makes it clear that what is required is something more than a general acknowledgement of a factual situation, but rather that the State identifies the conduct in question and makes it its own.

According to a Washington Post article of 17 April 2014:[157]

> In early March, Putin denied that the well-equipped troops operating on Ukraine's Crimean Peninsula and wearing green uniforms without insignia were Russian. Anyone could buy those uniforms, he said. On Thursday, when asked about the soldiers widely known as the green men, Putin acknowledged that they were Russian. Their presence had been necessary, he said, to keep order so that Crimeans could decide their future in a referendum.
>
> "We didn't want any tanks, any nationalist combat units or people with extreme views armed with automatic weapons," he said. "Of course, Russian servicemen backed the Crimean self-defense forces."
>
> The hastily arranged March 16 referendum resulted in 96 percent counted as voting for joining Russia. "In this situation," he said, "we couldn't have done otherwise."

[155] UN Doc. A/56/10, p. 52.

[156] Ibid. p. 53.

[157] 'Putin's remarks raise fears of future moves against Ukraine', Washington Post, 17 April 2014. https://www.washingtonpost.com/world/putin-changes-course-admits-russian-troops-were-in-crimea-before-vote/2014/04/17/b3300a54-c617-11e3-bf7a-be01a9b69cf1_story.html

It is not clear if this statement amounted to acknowledgment and adoption as Russia's own conduct,[158] but it should be noted that subsequent statements made by a senior government official of a State may reveal the attribution of the deployment of irregular armed forces to the State. These rules on attribution and ICJ's position on the standard of proof should be referred to when the State deploying armed forces tries to hide its involvement.[159]

References

Akande, D. & Tzanakopoulos, A. (2021). Legal: Use of Force in Self-Defence to Recover Occupied Territory. EJIL 32(4): 1299–1307

Asada, M. (2024). The War in Ukraine Under International Law: Its Use of Force and Armed Conflict Aspects, in *The War in Ukraine and International Law* ed. by Asada M, Tamada D, Springer

Brownlie, I. (1963). *International Law and the Use of Force by States*, Oxford University Press

Brunk, I. & Hakimi, M. (2024). The Prohibition of Annexations and the Foundations of Modern International Law. AJIL 118(3): 417–467

Corten, O. (2010). *The Law Against War, The Prohibition on the Use of Force in Contemporary International Law*. Hart

Corten, O. (2015). The Russian Intervention in the Ukrainian Crisis: Was Jus Contra Bellum Confirmed rather than Weakened. Journal on Use of Force & International Law. 2(1):17-41

Corten, O. (2020). The Prohibition of the Use of Force, in *The UN Friendly Relations Declaration at 50 An Assessment of the Fundamental Principles of International Law* ed. by Viñuales JE. Cambridge University Press

Dinstein, Y. (2010). *The Conduct of Hostilities under the Law of International Armed Conflict*, 2nd edn. Cambridge University Press

Dörr, O. & Randelzhofer, A. (2012). Article 2(4), in *The Charter of the United Nations: A Commentary*, 3rd edn. Voi. I. ed. by Simma B et al. Oxford University Press

Gray, C. (2006). The Eritrea/Ethiopia Claims Commission Oversteps Its Boundaries: A Partial Award? EJIL 17(4): 699–721

Hofmann, R. (2020). Annexation, in *Max Planck Encyclopaedia of Public International Law* (2020)

Hudson, M. (1933a). Verdict of the League: China and Japan in Manchuria: Official Documents with Notes and an Introduction. World Peace Foundation

Hudson, M. (1933b). The Report of the Assembly of the League of Nations on the Sino-Japanese Dispute. AJIL 27(2): 300–305.

Klein, P. & Koutroulis, V. (2018). Territorial disputes and the use of force, in *Research Handbook on Territorial Disputes in International Law* ed. by Kohen M, Hébié M. Edward Elgar

Korman, S. (1996). The Right of conquest: The Acquisition of Territory by Force in International Law and Practice, Clarendon Press Oxford

Mikanagi, T. & Ogi, H. (2016). The Japanese Views on Legal Issues Related to Security, Japanese Yearbook of International Law 59: 360–371

Mikanagi, T. (2018). Establishing a Military Presence in a Disputed Territory: Interpretation of Article 2(3) and (4) of the UN Charter, ICLQ 67(4): 1021–1034

[158] Reeves and Wallace consider that 'little green men' were confirmed to be members of the Russian Special Forces (Spetsnaz). Reeves and Wallace (2015), p. 378.

[159] Corten took a cautious approach in proving the attribution to Russia. Corten (2015), p. 20.

Mikanagi, T. & Mačák, K. (2020). Attribution of Cyber Operations: An International Law Perspective on the Park Jin Hyok Case. Cambridge International Law Journal 9(1): 51–75

Mikanagi, T. (2021). Application of the Due Diligence Principle to Cyber Operations. International Law Studies 97:1019–1038 https://digital-commons.usnwc.edu/cgi/viewcontent.cgi?article=2979&context=ils

Murphy, S. (2018). The Eritrean-Ethiopian War (1998–2000), in *The Use of Force in International Law: A Case-Based Approach* ed. by Corten O, Ruys T. Oxford University Press

O'Connell, M.E. (2018). The Crisis in Ukraine – 2014, in *The Use of Force in International Law: A Case-Based Approach*, ed. by Corten O, Ruys T. Oxford University Press

Pobjie, E. (2024). *Prohibited Force: The Meaning of 'Use of Force' in International Law*. Cambridge University Press

Reeves, S.R. & Wallace, D. (2015). The Combatant Status of the "Little Green Men" and Other Participants in the Ukraine Conflict. International Law Studies 91:361–401

Riddell, A. & Plant, B. (2009). Evidence before the International Court of Justice. BIICL

Ruys, T. (2014). The Meaning of "Force" and the Boundaries of the Jus ad Bellum: Are "Minimal" Use of Force Excluded from UN Charter Article 2(4)? AJIL 108(2):159–210

Ruys, T. & Silvestre, F.R. (2021a). Illegal: The Recourse to Force to Recover Occupied Territory and the Second Nagorno-Karabakh War. EJIL 32(4): 1287–1297

Ruys, T. & Silvestre, F.R. (2021b). Military Action to Recover Occupied Land: Lawful Self-defense or Prohibited Use of Force? The 2020 Nagorno-Karabakh Conflict Revisited. International Law Studies 97: 665–738 https://digital-commons.usnwc.edu/ils/vol97/iss1/31/

Shinkaretskaia, G.G. (1989). Peaceful Settlement of International Disputes: An Alternative to the Use of Force, in *The Non-Use of Force in International Law* ed. by Butler WE. Martinus Nijhoff

Tams, C. (2024). Article 2(4), in *The Charter of the United Nations, A Commentary*, 4th edn. Vol. I, ed. by Simma B et al. Oxford University Press

Tomuschat, C. (2024). Article 2(3), in *The Charter of the United Nations, A Commentary*, 4th edn. Vol. I, ed. by Simma B et al. Oxford University Press

Yiallourides, C., Gehring, M. & Gauci, J.P. (2018). The Use of Force in Relation to Sovereign Disputes over Land Territory. BIICL. https://www.biicl.org/publications/the-use-of-force-in-relation-to-sovereignty-disputes-over-land-territory

Chapter 4
Effect of the Prohibition of Acquisition of Territory by Force

4.1 Denial of the Acquisition of Territory by Use of Force in Self-Defence

4.1.1 The 1970 Friendly Relations Declaration

As mentioned in Sect. 2.1.2, the Stimson Doctrine was often explained to be based on the principle that an illegal act cannot give birth to a right in law (*ex injuria jus non oritur*). This explanation naturally leads to the following question: 'Does lawful use of force give birth to territorial title?' In the context of the development of international law since the establishment of the UN, this question can be paraphrased as: 'Does PATBF, which is a corollary of PUF under Article 2(4) of the UN Charter, have the effect of denying the acquisition of territorial title through use of force initiated as the exercise of the right to self-defence under Article 51 of the UN Charter?'

The Friendly Relations Declaration states: 'The territory of a State shall not be the object of acquisition by another State resulting from the threat or use of force … No territorial acquisition resulting from the threat or use of force shall be recognized as legal'. This part of the Declaration contains no exception for force used in self-defence and does not limit the application of PATBF to unlawful uses of force. By contrast, in the sentence immediately prior to the quoted part, the Declaration prohibits 'military occupation resulting from the use of force in contravention of the provisions of the Charter', indicating that where the use of force is not prohibited by the Charter, military occupation may be lawful. Thus, the 1970 Declaration strongly indicates that lawful use of force in self-defence cannot create territorial title.

T. Mikanagi, *Toward Stronger Rule of Law Against Attempts to Acquire Territory by Force*, SpringerBriefs in Law,
https://doi.org/10.1007/978-981-95-2814-1_4

4.1.2 Academic Literature

The interpretation of the 1970 Declaration above is supported by Akehust. He wrote as follows:[1]

> In these words, the Declaration makes a significant distinction between military occupation and acquisition of territory. Military occupation is unlawful only if it results from the use of force in contravention of the Charter; any threat or use of force, whether it is in contravention of the Charter or not, invalidates acquisition of territory.

In the oral statement made on behalf of Japan before the ICJ on the 2024 Advisory Opinion, based on the study on relevant academic literature, Professor Akande examined two alternative but interlinked logics supporting the position above and rejected the argument allowing acquisition of territorial title through lawful use of force. These were:

– The principle prohibiting acquisition of territory by force precludes any acquisition of territorial title through force, regardless of whether that force is unlawful or permitted as an exercise of self-defence.
– The uses of force resulting in the annexation of territory will never be lawful as exercises of self-defence since permanent annexation can never be a proportionate response to an armed attack.

The distinction between these two logics conceptually exists, but, as Professor Akande mentioned, they are interlinked and it is difficult to draw a clear line between them.

The language of the 1970 Declaration seems to fit the first of the two logics above. From a policy perspective, it can be pointed out that, if lawful use of force based on the right to self-defence can confer title upon a State, in practice, it would be liable to abuse.[2] The proper scope of self-defence in international law is controversial, and States frequently make contested claims that some use of force or another is lawful as an exercise of self-defence. States seeking to acquire territory by force could accordingly seek to exploit this ambiguity. This would threaten to undermine PATBF.[3] So, from this perspective, the possibility of acquiring territory by use of force in self-defence should be denied altogether. This might be one of the rationales for the language of the 1970 Declarations.

On the other hand, the second logic suggested by Professor Akande also seems to be valid. Jennings wrote in 1963: 'Force used in self-defence—whatever that may mean—is undoubtedly lawful. But it must be proportionate to the threat of immediate danger, and when the threat has been averted the plea of self-defence can no longer be available.' He further argued: 'it must still be said that it would be a curious law of self-defence that permitted the defender in the course of self-defence

[1] Akehurst (1987), p. 149. See also Klein and Koutroulis (2018), p. 239, Brunk and Hakimi (2024), p. 437.

[2] Jennings (1963), p. 55.

[3] Korman (1996), pp. 206–207.

that permitted the defender in the course of his defence to seize and keep the resources and territory of the attacker'.[4] Bowett also wrote in 1971: 'One can conceive of self-defence justifying the temporary occupation of territory but never the permanent acquisition of title, and there is no system or principle of law which conceives of such a thing'.[5]

Regarding Jenning's use of the term 'curious', Sharon Korman pointed out that, for a State which has repeatedly been a victim of aggression, the law of self-defence allowing annexation of a territory of an aggressor used for a base for attacks is not altogether curious. However, she also wrote: 'Yet the view urged by Jennings and Bowett does appear tenable if it is argued that is it not the notion of self-defence as such … but rather the singularly limited scope of that concept in the context of the United Nations Charter, which precludes the acquisition of territory by conquest as a result of action taken under Article 51'. She further explains: 'That a policy based on self-defence within the terms of Article 51 would, in principle, seek the restoration (or preservation) of the status quo rather than territorial gain, follows, then, from the meaning of self-defence as forcible action taken in response to the initiation of an armed attack, which is to be distinguished from a use of force designed to provide safety against future attacks'.[6]

This conclusion seems convincing. The exercise of the right to self-defence must be proportionate to the armed attack and necessary to respond to it.[7] Self-defence, by definition, can only justify the taking of temporary measures in order to achieve its aims. The aim of self-defence is limited to defending the attacked State and its people. Thus, even when a State has suffered an armed attack, it can never be proportionate to permanently deprive a people of its territory.[8]

4.1.3 Security Council Resolutions

As discussed earlier, Security Council resolution 242 emphasised 'the inadmissibility of the acquisition of territory by war' without drawing any distinction between lawful and unlawful uses of force.[9] In the case of the Iraqi invasion of Kuwait in 1990, the acquisition of territory by force was denied for Kuwait acting in self-defence. In the Security Council resolution 686 (1991), while demanding that Iraq 'rescind immediately its actions', the Security Council simultaneously affirmed 'the commitment of all Member States to the independence, sovereignty and territorial

---

[4] Jennings (1963), p. 55. Jennings and Watts (1992), p. 704.

[5] Bowett (1971), p. 475.

[6] Korman (1996), pp. 203–205.

[7] Legality of the Threat or Use of Nuclear Weapons, Advisory Opinion, 8 July 1996, ICJ Rep. (1996), p. 245, para. 41. The Nicaragua judgment, p. 94, para. 176. The Oil Platforms judgment, p. 183, para. 43.

[8] O'Meara (2021), p. 139.

[9] Korman (1996), p. 212

integrity of Iraq and Kuwait'. It is thus clear that the territory of Iraq had not become liable to annexation even if States were to act in defence of Kuwait.[10]

4.1.4 *The 2024 Advisory Opinion*

In the 2024 Advisory Opinion, as quoted earlier, the ICJ found that: 'to seek to acquire sovereignty over an occupied territory, as shown by the policies and practices adopted by Israel in East Jerusalem and the West Bank, is contrary to the prohibition of the use of force in international relations and its corollary principle of the non-acquisition of territory by force'. The Court also said as follows:

> 253. The Court observes that an occupation involves, by its very nature, a continued use of force in foreign territory. Such use of force is, however, subject to the rules of international law governing the legality of the use of force or jus ad bellum. As indicated in Part V.C. above, these rules prohibit the use of force to acquire territory. Under contemporary international law as contained in the Charter of the United Nations and reflected in customary international law, occupation can under no circumstances serve as the source of title to territory or justify its acquisition by the occupying Power.
> 254. Israel's assertion of sovereignty over and its annexation of certain parts of the territory constitute, as shown above, a violation of the prohibition of the acquisition of territory by force. This violation has a direct impact on the legality of Israel's continued presence, as an occupying Power, in the Occupied Palestinian Territory. The Court considers that Israel is not entitled to sovereignty over or to exercise sovereign powers in any part of the Occupied Palestinian Territory on account of its occupation. Nor can Israel's security concerns override the principle of the prohibition of the acquisition of territory by force.

These paragraphs, especially the use of terms such as 'under no circumstances' in paragraph 253 and the denial of justification based on 'security concerns' in paragraph 254, strongly indicate that the Court denies acquisition of territory by occupation, which involves use of force, under any circumstances, including in exercising the right to self-defence.

The Joint Declaration of Judges Nolte and Cleveland on this Advisory Opinion explains as follows:[11]

> 7. On the other hand, as the Court explains, the threat or use of force to seek to permanently acquire territory is prohibited — indeed, it is absolutely prohibited. The right of self-defence can never justify the acquisition of territory by force, including such use of force for the protection of perceived security interests. Such acts are strictly prohibited by the United Nations Charter and by customary international law.

The Separate Opinion of Judge Iwasawa also explains:[12]

> The prohibition of the acquisition of territory by force precludes any forcible acquisition of territory, regardless of whether that force is unlawful or otherwise permitted under

---

[10] Korman (1996), p. 215.

[11] Joint Declaration of Judge Nolte and Cleveland, the 2024 ICJ Advisory Opinion, para. 7.

[12] Separate Opinion of Judge Iwasawa, the 2024 ICJ Advisory Opinion, para. 15.

> international law. Israel's policies and practices amount to the annexation of large parts of the Occupied Palestinian Territory and thus violate the prohibition of the acquisition of territory by force (para. 179).

The Declaration of Judge Charlesworth also argues that annexation is incompatible with justification based on the right to self-defence:[13]

> In addition to this, however, such conduct belies the proposition that Israel's effective control of the Occupied Palestinian Territory is a permissible use of force in self-defence. The assertion of permanent control over foreign territory is incompatible with the aim of preserving a State's territorial integrity, which is one of the key justifications for the right to self-defence. Rather than preserving the integrity of its territory, a State using force to annex foreign territory seeks to expand it at the expense of the local government.

These judges clarify that the Court's denial of acquisition of territory through occupation includes acquisition of territory through occupation in exercising the right to self-defence.

Based on these considerations, it seems reasonable to conclude that PATBF has the effect of denying the acquisition of territorial title through use of force initiated as the exercise of the right to self-defence under Article 51 of the UN Charter. As mentioned in Sect. 3.1 above, in paragraph 179 of the 2024 Advisory Opinion the ICJ found that 'to seek to acquire sovereignty over an occupied territory, as shown by the policies and practices adopted by Israel in East Jerusalem and the West Bank, is contrary to the prohibition of the use of force in international relations and its corollary principle of the non-acquisition of territory by force.' In this paragraph, the ICJ seems to take the position that, even if the occupation of territory has started as the lawful exercise of the right to self-defence, once the occupying power seeks to acquire sovereignty over the occupied territory, it would violate both PUF and PATBF. Therefore, this paragraph seems to indicate that the violation of PATBF does not have to be preceded by the violation of PUF. If a State occupies an area of land which is not within its internationally recognised territory nor under its existing administration and which is another State's internationally recognised territory or territory likely to be another State's territory through unlawful use of force, and later attempts to annex it, this attempt to annex the area will violate PATBF, and this violation of PATBF will be preceded by the violation of PUF. On the other hand, even if a State occupies such an area through lawful use of force based on its right to self-defence, once it starts to annex the territory, it will violate both PATBF and PUF.

As mentioned above, in February 2022, Russia sent a letter to the UN informing of the measures taken in accordance with Article 51 of the UN Charter, and this letter shows Russia's intention to rely on the right of collective self-defence for the two Donbas 'Republics'. When the UNGA adopted ES-11/4 on 13 October 2022, 143 States supported it but 50 States did not. The 2024 ICJ Advisory Opinion should provide good basis for the latter States to consider if what the Court said in paragraphs 253 and 254 of the Opinion quoted above applies to Russian attempts to

[13] Declaration of Judge Cleveland, the 2024 ICJ Advisory Opinion, para. 26.

acquire Ukraine's territory. According to the Court, under contemporary international law as contained in the Charter of the United Nations and reflected in customary international law, occupation can under no circumstances, including occupation resulting from alleged invocation of right of collective self-defence, serve as the source of title to territory or justify its acquisition by the occupying Power. For strengthening rule of law against attempts to acquire territory by force, double standards in the application of law must be avoided, and paragraphs 253 and 254 of the 2024 Advisory Opinion should be accepted as a single standard applicable not only to the OPT but also to Ukraine.

4.2 Obligations for Third States

The 1970 Declaration provides: 'No territorial acquisition resulting from the threat or use of force shall be recognized as legal.' The violation of PATBF has the effect of imposing obligations on third States not to recognise territorial acquisition resulting from the use of force as legal. As will be examined below, the 2024 ICJ Advisory Opinion seems to have recognised obligations for third States beyond the obligation not to recognise.

The existence of obligations for third States requires them to take a cautious approach to potential attempts to acquire territory by force and warns them against premature recognition of the acquisition of territory as legal. In a system where central enforcement and judicial authorities are weak, decentralised mechanisms of pressure from constituent entities need to play an important role in ensuring the observance of law. Such pressure must also be exerted in accordance with international law, and the clarification of law relating to the third States's obligation emanating from the violation of PATBF should have the effect of strengthening the rule of law.

4.2.1 Obligations Erga Omnes *and* Jus Cogens

In the 2024 Advisory Opinion, the ICJ confirmed that not only the obligation to respect the right of Palestinian people to self-determination but also the obligation arising from PATBF is an obligation *erga omnes*.[14] In this Opinion, the ICJ did not determine that PATBF is a peremptory norm (*jus cogens*), and it simply said that it is an obligation *erga omnes*. The obligation owed to the international community as a whole in Article 48(1)(b) of the ILC's Articles on State Responsibility is obligation *erga omnes*. This article provides:

Article 48 Invocation of responsibility by a State other than an injured State

[14] The 2024 ICJ Advisory Opinion, para. 274.

> 1. Any State other than an injured State is entitled to invoke the responsibility of another State in accordance with paragraph 2 if:
> (a) the obligation breached is owed to a group of States including that State, and is established for the protection of a collective interest of the group; or
> (b) the obligation breached is owed to the international community as a whole.

The ILC's commentary on Article 48(1)(b) explains the relationship between Article 48 (1)(b) and obligations *erga omnes* as follows:[15]

> (8) Under *paragraph 1* (b), States other than the injured State may invoke responsibility if the obligation in question was owed "to the international community as a whole". The provision intends to give effect to the statement by ICJ in the *Barcelona Traction* case, where the Court drew "an essential distinction" between obligations owed to particular States and those owed "towards the international community as a whole". With regard to the latter, the Court went on to state that "[i]n view of the importance of the rights involved, all States can be held to have a legal interest in their protection; they are obligations *erga omnes*".

As examples of obligations *erga omnes*, this ILC commentary refers to aggression, but not to PATBF as such. The commentary reads as follows:[16]

> (9) ... Nor is it the function of the articles to provide a list of those obligations which under existing international law are owed to the international community as a whole. This would go well beyond the task of codifying the secondary rules of State responsibility, and in any event, such a list would be only of limited value, as the scope of the concept will necessarily evolve over time. The Court itself has given useful guidance: in its 1970 judgment it referred, by way of example, to "the outlawing of acts of aggression, and of genocide" and to "the principles and rules concerning the basic rights of the human person, including protection from slavery and racial discrimination". In its judgment in the *East Timor* case, the Court added the right of self-determination of peoples to this list.

The commentary on Chapter III of the Articles on State Responsibility explains the relationship between peremptory norms (*jus cogens*) and obligations *erga omnes* as follows:[17]

> Whether or not peremptory norms of general international law and obligations to the international community as a whole are aspects of a single basic idea, there is at the very least substantial overlap between them. The examples which ICJ has given of obligations towards the international community as a whole all concern obligations which, it is generally accepted, arise under peremptory norms of general international law. Likewise the examples of peremptory norms given by the Commission in its commentary to what became article 53 of the 1969 Vienna Convention involve obligations to the international community as a whole. But there is at least a difference in emphasis. While peremptory norms of general international law focus on the scope and priority to be given to a certain number of fundamental obligations, the focus of obligations to the international community as a whole is essentially on the legal interest of all States in compliance—i.e. in terms of the present articles, in being entitled to invoke the responsibility of any State in breach.

[15] UN Doc. A/56/10, p. 127.

[16] Ibid.

[17] Ibid. pp. 111–112.

With regard to the relationship between aggression and unlawful use of force, the 1986 ICJ Nicaragua judgment explains their difference as follows:[18]

> 191. As regards certain particular aspects of the principle in question, it will be necessary to distinguish the most grave forms of the use of force (those constituting an armed attack) from other less grave forms. In determining the legal rule which applies to these latter forms, the Court can again draw on the formulations contained in the Declaration on Principles of International Law concerning Friendly Relations and Co-operation among States in accordance with the Charter of the United Nations (General Assembly resolution 2625 (XXV), referred to above). As already observed, the adoption by States of this text affords an indication of their *opinio juris* as to customary international law on the question. Alongside certain descriptions which may refer to aggression, this text includes others which refer only to less grave forms of the use of force. In particular, according to this resolution:
>
> > "Every State has the duty to refrain from the threat or use of force to violate the existing international boundaries of another State or as a means of solving international disputes, including territorial disputes and problems concerning frontiers of States.
>
> ...
>
> > States have a duty to refrain from acts of reprisal involving the use of force.
>
> ...
>
> > Every State has the duty to refrain from any forcible action which deprives peoples referred to in the elaboration of the principle of equal rights and self-determination of that right to self-determination and freedom and independence.
> > Every State has the duty to refrain from organizing or encouraging the organization of irregular forces or armed bands, including mercenaries, for incursion into the territory of another State.
> > Every State has the duty to refrain from organizing, instigating, assisting or participating in acts of civil strife or terrorist acts in another State or acquiescing in organized activities within its territory directed towards the commission of such acts, when the acts referred to in the present paragraph involve a threat or use of force."

The Court, therefore, indicates that use of force prohibited by Article 2(4) has a most grave form, which is equivalent to aggression, and less grave forms. A non-exhaustive list of *jus cogens* annexed to the ILC's 'Draft conclusions on identification and legal consequences of peremptory norms of general international law (*jus cogens*)'[19] refers to aggression but not PATBF or PUF. If acquisition of territory by force involves the most grave form of use of force, or aggression, it would violate *jus cogens*. The definition of aggression is still controversial, but at least theoretically it is possible that acquisition of territory by the less grave form of use of force does not amount to the violation of *jus cogens*.

The particular significance of PATBF compared with PUF lies in its function in denying the acquisition of territorial title through use of force and this particular significance may give additional gravity to the violation of PATBF. This additional gravity might contribute to the designation of PATBF as a peremptory norm (*jus cogens*), but it is not yet clear. Even in a case of acquisition of territory by force which does not amount to the violation of *jus cogens*, considering the ICJ's view that the obligation arising from PATBF is an obligation *erga omnes*, even the

[18] The Nicaragua judgment, para. 191.

[19] UN Doc. A/77/10.

acquisition of territory by a less grave form of use of force, if such a form exists, should amount to the violation of obligation *erga omnes*.

4.2.2 Obligations for Third States Mentioned in the 2024 ICJ Opinion

In the 2024 Advisory Opinion, the ICJ elaborated on the duties for third States. The relevant paragraphs read as follows:[20]

> 278. Taking note of the resolutions of the Security Council and General Assembly, the Court is of the view that Member States are under an obligation not to recognize any changes in the physical character or demographic composition, institutional structure or status of the territory occupied by Israel on 5 June 1967, including East Jerusalem, except as agreed by the parties through negotiations and to distinguish in their dealings with Israel between the territory of the State of Israel and the Palestinian territory occupied since 1967. The Court considers that the duty of distinguishing dealings with Israel between its own territory and the Occupied Palestinian Territory encompasses, inter alia, the obligation to abstain from treaty relations with Israel in all cases in which it purports to act on behalf of the Occupied Palestinian Territory or a part thereof on matters concerning the Occupied Palestinian Territory or a part of its territory; to abstain from entering into economic or trade dealings with Israel concerning the Occupied Palestinian Territory or parts thereof which may entrench its unlawful presence in the territory; to abstain, in the establishment and maintenance of diplomatic missions in Israel, from any recognition of its illegal presence in the Occupied Palestinian Territory; and to take steps to prevent trade or investment relations that assist in the maintenance of the illegal situation created by Israel in the Occupied Palestinian Territory (see Legal Consequences for States of the Continued Presence of South Africa in Namibia (South West Africa) notwithstanding Security Council Resolution 276 (1970), Advisory Opinion, I.C.J. Reports 1971, pp. 55–56, paras. 122, 125–127).
> 279. Moreover, the Court considers that, in view of the character and importance of the rights and obligations involved, all States are under an obligation not to recognize as legal the situation arising from the unlawful presence of Israel in the Occupied Palestinian Territory. They are also under an obligation not to render aid or assistance in maintaining the situation created by Israel's illegal presence in the Occupied Territory.

According to the ICJ's categorisation, there are two kinds of obligations with four subcategories of the latter:

Obligation A: An obligation not to recognise any changes in the physical character or demographic composition, institutional structure or status of the OPT except as agreed by the parties through negotiations;

Obligation B: An obligation to distinguish in their dealings with Israel between the territory of the State of Israel and the OPT;

(i) An obligation to abstain from treaty relations with Israel in all cases in which it purports to act on behalf of the OPT or a part thereof on matters concerning the OPT or a part of its territory;

[20] The 2024 ICJ Advisory Opinion, paras. 278–279.

(ii) An obligation to abstain from entering into economic or trade dealings with Israel concerning the OPT or parts thereof which may entrench its unlawful presence in the territory;
(iii) An obligation to abstain, in the establishment and maintenance of diplomatic missions in Israel, from any recognition of its illegal presence in the OPT; and
(iv) An obligation to take steps to prevent trade or investment relations that assist in the maintenance of the illegal situation created by Israel in the OPT.

4.2.3 Obligations Not to Recognise and Not to Render Aid or Assistance

Article 41(2) of the ILC's Articles on State Responsibility refers to two types of obligations arising from a serious breach of obligations under peremptory norms of general international law (*jus cogens*), namely (a) obligation not to recognise as lawful a situation created, and (b) obligation not to render aid or assistance in maintaining that situation.[21] On the type (a) obligation, its commentary explains that this obligation applies to 'situations' created by the breaches, and it not only refers to the formal recognition of these situations but also prohibits acts which would 'imply' such recognition.[22] Obligation A above more or less corresponds to the formal recognition of situations created by breaches, and Obligation B (i) and (iii) seem to more or less correspond to implicit recognition.

On the type (b) obligation, the ILC's commentary explains that it may be seen as a logical extension of the duty of non-recognition but it has a separate scope of application insofar as actions concerned would not imply recognition of the situation created by breaches.[23] Obligation B (ii) above refers to entering into economic or trade dealings with Israel concerning OPT or parts thereof which may 'entrench' its unlawful presence. This seems to be a type (b) obligation for third State not to render aid or assistance.

Paragraph 278 of the 2024 Advisory Opinion refers to paragraph 122 of the Advisory Opinion on Legal Consequences for States of the Continued Presence of South Africa in Namibia (South West Africa) notwithstanding Security Council Resolution 276 (1970) (the 1971 Namibia Advisory Opinion). The ICJ said in paragraph 122:[24]

[21] UN Doc. A/56/10, p. 117.

[22] Ibid. p. 114 (5). Tams (2024), p. 363.

[23] UN Doc. A/56/10, p. 115 (12). Tams (2024), pp. 363–364.

[24] Legal Consequences for States of the Continued Presence of South Africa in Namibia (South West Africa) notwithstanding Security Council Resolution 276 (1970), Advisory Opinion, 21 June 1971, ICJ Rep. (1971) [hereinafter cited as the 1971 Namibia Advisory Opinion], p. 55, para. 122.

> member States are under obligation to abstain from entering into treaty relations with South Africa in all cases in which the Government of South Africa purports to act on behalf of or concerning Namibia. With respect to existing bilateral treaties, member States must abstain from invoking or applying those treaties or provisions of treaties concluded by South Africa on behalf of or concerning Namibia which involve active intergovernmental co-operation.

The obligation mentioned here is similar to obligation B (i) above, and, in this 1971 Namibia Advisory Opinion, the Court does not seem to be referring to the type (b) obligation, which is mentioned in Article 41(2) of the ILC's Articles on State Responsibility.

It seems significant that, in the 2024 Advisory Opinion, the ICJ recognised the existence of the type (b) obligation, namely, obligation not to render aid or assistance in maintaining the situation created by the violation of PATBF. As the ILC explained in the commentary on Article 41(2), this is an obligation separate from the obligation not to recognise.

Paragraph 278 of the 2024 Advisory Opinion talks about obligations for UN Member States and paragraph 279 talks about obligations for all States. Paragraph 279 refers to both (a) the obligation not to recognise as legal the situation arising from the unlawful presence of Israel in the OPT and (b) the obligation not to render aid or assistance in maintaining the situation created by Israel's illegal presence in the OPT. Therefore, the ICJ recognised a wider obligation for third States than obligation not to recognise in the 1971 Namibia Advisory Opinion.

4.2.4 Positive Obligation to Take Steps for Prevention

Obligation B(iv) is different from Obligation B(ii) in the sense that it does not concern aid or assistance rendered by a State itself. As it refers to prevention, it is the obligation for third States to prevent private actors from engaging in trade or investment relations that assist in the maintenance of the illegal situation created by Israel in the OPT. Article 41(2) refers to States' obligation not to render aid or assistance in maintaining that situation, and Obligation B(iv) seems to go beyond Article 41(2). Paragraph 279 of the 2024 Advisory Opinion, which talks about obligation for States in general rather than UN Member States, does not refer to this kind of obligation, and the Court seems to recognise a wider obligation for UN Member States than for other States.

This difference between paragraph 278 and 279 appears to be due to the consideration of the resolutions of the Security Council and the GA mentioned at the beginning of paragraph 278.

Earlier in paragraph 275, the Court said that, with regard to the right to self-determination, all States must co-operate with the United Nations to put into effect the modalities required to ensure an end to Israel's illegal presence in the OPT and the full realisation of the right of the Palestinian people to self-determination. The Court recalled the reference to the duty to cooperate to promote the realisation of the right to self-determination in the 1970 Declaration.

Next, in paragraph 276 the Court recalled Security Council resolutions relating to PATBF. The Court noted:[25]

- Security Council resolution 465 (1980) which determined that "all measures taken by Israel to change the physical character, demographic composition, institutional structure or status of the Palestinian and other Arab territories occupied since 1967, including Jerusalem, or any part thereof have no legal validity".
- Security Council in resolution 2334 (2016) which called upon "all States, bearing in mind paragraph 1 of this resolution, to distinguish, in their relevant dealings, between the territory of the State of Israel and the territories occupied since 1967".

In paragraph 277, the court noted GA resolutions relating to PATBF. The Court noted:[26]

- General Assembly resolution 74/11 (2019), which called upon all States "(a) Not to recognize any changes to the pre-1967 borders, including with regard to Jerusalem, other than those agreed by the parties through negotiations, including by ensuring that agreements with Israel do not imply recognition of Israeli sovereignty over the territories occupied by Israel in 1967; (b) To distinguish, in their relevant dealings, between the territory of the State of Israel and the territories occupied since 1967; (c) Not to render aid or assistance to illegal settlement activities, including not to provide Israel with any assistance to be used specifically in connection with settlements in the occupied territories, in line with Security Council resolution 465 (1980) of 1 March 1980; (d) To respect and ensure respect for international law, in all circumstances, including through measures of accountability, consistent with international law".
- General Assembly resolution 77/126, which called upon "all States, consistent with their obligations under international law and the relevant resolutions, not to recognize, and not to render aid or assistance in maintaining, the situation created by measures that are illegal under international law, including those aimed at advancing annexation in the Occupied Palestinian Territory, including East Jerusalem, and other Arab territories occupied by Israel since 1967";
- General Assembly resolution 32/161 (1977), which called upon "all States, international organizations, specialized agencies, investment corporations and all other institutions not to recognize, or cooperate with or assist in any manner, any measures undertaken by Israel to exploit the resources of the occupied territories or to effect any changes in the demographic composition or geographic character or institutional structure of those territories".

The Security Council and GA resolutions quoted by the Court in these paragraphs refer to obligation not to recognise (similar to Obligation A above), obligation to distinguish (similar to Obligation B (i) above), and obligation not to render aid or

[25] The 2024 ICJ Advisory Opinion, para.276.

[26] Ibid. para. 277.

assistance (similar to Obligation B (ii) and (iii) above), but it is not clear if there is any reference to obligation to 'take steps to prevent trade or investment relations' (Obligation B (iv) above).

On this matter, the Declaration of President Salam of the ICJ on the 2024 Advisory Opinion casts some light. In referring to Article 41 of the ILC's Articles on State Responsibility, he argues:[27]

> Consequently, with respect to Israeli policies and practices that infringe the Palestinian people's right to self-determination, all States are bound by the customary obligations laid down in that Article. This requires not only taking no action that might hinder the exercise of that right, but also providing the necessary lawful support for the realization of that right and co-operating actively with the United Nations to that end.

President Salem further argues:[28]

> 47. As our esteemed late colleague, James Crawford, wrote, it is important to note that the obligation to ensure respect is not satisfied by mere diplomatic protests ... or solely by co-operating with the United Nations. Indeed, as the Court has emphasized with regard to the crime of genocide, a State's referral of a violation of obligations *erga omnes* to the organs of the United Nations does not relieve other States of their obligations "to take such action as they can" to ensure respect for those obligations and prevent or punish violations thereof, "while respecting the United Nations Charter and any decisions that may have been taken by its competent organs" (see Application of the Convention on the Prevention and Punishment of the Crime of Genocide (Bosnia and Herzegovina v. Serbia and Montenegro), Judgment, I.C.J. Reports 2007 (I), p. 220, para. 427).

His reference to 'ensure respect for those obligation' seems to suggest that there is connection between obligation B(iv) and GA resolution 74/11 (2019) quoted in paragraph 177 of the Advisory Opinion, which refers to '(d) To respect and ensure respect for international law, in all circumstances, including through measures of accountability, consistent with international law'.

Article 41(1) of the ILC's Articles on State Responsibility provides: 'States shall cooperate to bring to an end through lawful means any serious breach within the meaning of article 40'.[29] Its commentary on Article 41(1) explains that this provision may reflect the progressive development of international law. The relevant part of the commentary reads:[30]

> Such cooperation must be through lawful means, the choice of which will depend on the circumstances of the given situation. It is, however, made clear that the obligation to cooperate applies to States whether or not they are individually affected by the serious breach. What is called for in the face of serious breaches is a joint and coordinated effort by all States to counteract the effects of these breaches. It may be open to question whether general international law at present prescribes a positive duty of cooperation, and paragraph 1 in that respect may reflect the progressive development of international law. But in fact such cooperation, especially in the framework of international organizations, is carried out

[27] Declaration of President Salem, the 2024 ICJ Advisory Opinion, para. 44.

[28] Ibid. para. 47.

[29] Article 40 refers to 'a serious breach by a State of an obligation arising under peremptory norms of general international law'.

[30] UN Doc. A/56/10, p. 114 (3)

> already in response to the gravest breaches of international law and it is often the only way of providing an effective remedy.

On the other hand, on this 'positive duty of cooperation', Conclusion 19 of the 'Draft conclusions on identification and legal consequences of peremptory norms of international law (jus cogens)' adopted by the ILC also refers to a similar obligation in its paragraph 1:[31]

> **Conclusion 19** Particular consequences of serious breaches of peremptory norms of general international law (jus cogens)
>
> 1. States shall cooperate to bring to an end through lawful means any serious breach by a State of an obligation arising under a peremptory norm of general international law (jus cogens).
>
> 2. No State shall recognize as lawful a situation created by a serious breach by a State of an obligation arising under a peremptory norm of general international law (jus cogens), nor render aid or assistance in maintaining that situation.
>
> 3. A breach of an obligation arising under a peremptory norm of general international law (jus cogens) is serious if it involves a gross or systematic failure by the responsible State to fulfil that obligation.
>
> 4. This draft conclusion is without prejudice to the other consequences that any breach by a State of an obligation arising under a peremptory norm of general international law (jus cogens) may entail under international law.

The commentary on Conclusion 19 of the 'Draft conclusions on identification and legal consequences of peremptory norms of international law (jus cogens)', which is drafted by Professor Dire Tladi, who is now a judge of the ICJ, differs from the commentary on Article 41(1) of the Articles on State Responsibility as follows:[32]

> ... the obligation to cooperate to bring to an end serious breaches of obligations arising under peremptory norms of general international law (jus cogens) is now recognized under international law.

Judge Tladi explained in his declaration on the 2024 Advisory Opinion as follows:[33]

> 31. The *erga omnes* character of the obligations does not itself create obligation on third States. A point that was articulated by Judge Higgins in her separate opinion appended to the Wall Advisory Opinion, where she expressed her disagreement with the Court's position that the consequences specified in the Opinion for the identified violations of international law (in paras. 154–159) flowed from the *erga omnes* character of the obligations breached. In her view, the *erga omnes* concept concerns "jurisdictional locus standi", which "has nothing to do with imposing substantive obligations on third parties". She thus concluded that the consequences specified by the Court did not "have anything to do with the concept of *erga omnes*", and that "[t]he obligation upon United Nations Members of non-recognition and non-assistance [did] not rest on the notion of *erga omnes*". This is precisely why there is virtually no support for the view that the *erga omnes* character of the obligation also gives rise to the consequences identified in Article 41 of the ILC's Articles on State Responsibility. It should be recalled that not all *erga omnes* obligations derive from peremptory norms. Obligations arising from customary international law norms concerning common spaces, for example, also have an *erga omnes* character whether they flow from peremptory norms

[31] UN Doc. A/77/10, p. 70.

[32] UN Doc. A/77/10, p. 77.

[33] Declaration of Judge Tladi, the 2024 ICJ Advisory Opinion, para. 31.

> or not. Without ruling out the possibility, it is not at all clear to me that all obligations having an *erga omnes* character produce the threefold duties of non-recognition, non-assistance and co-operation as formulated in Article 41 of the Articles on State Responsibility. It is possible that they do, but it is not at all clear that this is the case. What is clear, however, is that peremptory norms do. Accordingly, for the sake of sound and coherent judicial reasoning, the Court ought to have tied explicitly the Article 41 consequences identified for third States in this Opinion to the peremptory status of the right of self-determination (or even better, explicitly reaffirmed the peremptory character of other norms discussed in the Opinion).

President Salem and Judge Tladi focus on the right to self-determination as a norm from which the duty to cooperate emanates, and Judge Tladi seems to consider that the duty to cooperate referred to as obligation B(iv) above arises not from the violation of obligation *erga omnes*, but from the violation of peremptory norms (*jus cogens*). On the other hand, if at least more serious cases of acquisition of territory by force may amount to violation of peremptory norm, they may impose on third States the duty to cooperate through taking steps to prevent trade or investment relations that assist the maintenance of the illegal situation created by the unlawful acquisition of territory by force in accordance with the logic in paragraph 278 of the 2024 Advisory Opinion.

Obligation B(iv) above is an obligation to 'take steps to prevent trade or investment relations that assist in the maintenance of the illegal situation created by Israel in the OPT'. It is an obligation to prevent certain activities of private actors in the areas of trade and investment. As private actors generally have freedom in these economic activities, this kind of obligation seems likely to have the nature of 'due diligence' obligation. With regard to the concept of the due diligence obligation, the 1872 Alabama Arbitral Award held that 'due diligence' ought to be exercised by neutral governments in exact proportion to the risks to which either of the belligerents may be exposed, from a failure to fulfil the obligations of neutrality on their part;[34] and, in the 2007 Genocide Convention (Bosnia and Herzegovina v. Serbia and Montenegro) case, the ICJ seems to consider the nature of the obligation to prevent genocide under the Genocide Convention to be the due diligence obligation of the contracting States to exercise the capacity to influence the actions of persons likely to commit genocide to prevent genocide so far as possible.[35]

If these views expressed by the tribunals on obligations for States to prevent some activities in their territory, which were regarded as 'due diligence' obligations, are taken into account, Obligation B(iv) above should impose obligation upon Member States proportionate to the risks entailed in the relevant trade or investment relations of actors under their national jurisdictions in assisting the maintenance of the illegal situation created by the occupying power, and within their respective capacities. For example, if the contribution of certain trade or investment relations

---

[34] Alabama claims of the United States of America against Great Britain, Award,14 September 1872, the tribunal of arbitration established by Article I of the Treaty of Washington of 8 May 1871, RIAA 29, p. 129.

[35] The Bosnia Genocide judgment, p. 221, para. 430. See also Mikanagi (2021), pp. 1031–34.

to the maintenance of the illegal situation created by occupying power in the occupied territory is not significant, the obligation to take steps to prevent such trade or investment should decrease accordingly. In addition, third States are not obliged to take measures beyond their respective capacities to prevent such trade or investment. Therefore, the contents of Obligation B(iv) depend upon the capacities of implementing States and the assessment of risks entailed.

Resolution ES-11/1 entitled 'Aggression against Ukraine' was adopted by the GA on 2 March 2022 with 141 votes in favour. On 12 October 2022, the GA adopted Resolution ES-11/4 condemning Russia's attempt to annex parts of Ukraine with 143 votes in favour. These numbers seem to indicate the broad recognition of the unlawfulness of Russia's attempt to annex parts of Ukraine. Although these resolutions were adopted with an overwhelming majority, the absence of a legally binding Security Council resolution caused a mixed response to the GA resolutions. Some States, mainly Western States, took measures not to give permission for transfer of certain assets in their territories and imposed trade, travel and other restrictions, but other States did not.

The Security Council has primary responsibility for the maintenance of international peace and security. However, if the Security Council, because of lack of unanimity among the permanent members, fails to exercise its primary responsibility in a case where there appears to be a threat to peace, breach of the peace, or act of aggression, the GA may make recommendations to Members for the maintenance of international peace and security under the Uniting for Peace resolution.

The commentary on Conclusion 19 of the ILC's Draft Conclusion on Jus Cogens explains:[36]

> There are numerous examples of resolutions of organs of international organizations, in particular the United Nations, that illustrate the duty to cooperate to bring to an end serious breaches of obligations that are widely recognized as arising from peremptory norms of general international law (jus cogens). These include resolutions condemning breaches of such obligations, resolutions calling for the cessation of breaches of such obligations, and resolutions establishing accountability mechanisms to address such breaches.

It also refers to GA resolution ES-11/1 of 2 March 2022 in the footnotes.

If this explanation is correct and the obligation to 'take steps to prevent trade or investment relations that assist in the maintenance of the illegal situation created' by occupying power in occupied territory mentioned in paragraph 278 of the ICJ's 2024 Advisory Opinion emanates from the violation of *jus cogens* as Judges Salem and Tladi argued in their opinions, third States might have a similar obligation with regard to Russia's attempt to acquire Ukrainian territory.

As discussed above, the contents of the obligation for States should depend upon their capacities and the assessment of risks entailed. In implementing this obligation, States also need to examine the legality of the measures under other rules of international law. Such other rules of international law would include rules of international agreements in the area of trade and investment.

---

[36] UN Doc. A/77/10, p74, n. 250, 251.

The legality of measures under these other rules of international law needs to be determined on a case-by-case basis taking applicable rules of international law into account. On the other hand, the existence of the obligation to take steps to prevent trade or investment relations that assist in the maintenance of the illegal situation created by the violation of PATBF shall be taken into account in interpreting other applicable international agreements as a relevant rule of international law in the relations between the parties,[37] and may be taken into account in the identification of relevant rules of customary international law based on the ICJ's opinion on this obligation in the 2024 Advisory Opinion.[38]

4.2.5 Five Obligations and Application to the Scenarios

Based on the foregoing analysis, the following obligations are likely to arise from the violation of PATBF.

Obligation 1: Not to recognise change in status
An obligation not to recognise any changes in the physical character or demographic composition, institutional structure or status of the territory made by the deploying State;

Obligation 2: Not to recognise through diplomatic missions
An obligation to abstain, in the establishment and maintenance of diplomatic missions in the deploying State, from any recognition of its illegal presence in the territory in question;

Obligation 3: Not to recognise through treaty
An obligation to abstain from treaty relations with the deploying State in all cases in which it purports to act on behalf of the territory in question or a part thereof on matters concerning the territory in question or a part thereof;

Obligation 4: Not to render aid or assistance through economic or trade dealings
An obligation to abstain from entering into economic or trade dealings with the deploying State concerning the territory in question or parts thereof which may entrench its unlawful presence in the territory;

Obligation 5: To cooperate through preventing trade or investment relations rendering assistance
An obligation to take steps to prevent trade or investment relations that assist in the maintenance of the illegal situation created by the deploying State in the territory in question. (Note: This obligation might arise only when the violation of acquisition of territory by force involves the violation of peremptory norm, including when use of force involved in the attempt to acquisition of territory amounts to aggression.)

---

[37] See Article 31(3)(c) of the Vienna Convention of Law of Treaties

[38] See Conclusion 13 (Decisions of courts and tribunals) of the ILC's Draft conclusions on identification of customary international law (UN Doc. A/73/10, p.149).

In the Scenarios in Sect. 3.4 above, third States should take the following actions to avoid violation of the obligations arising from the deploying State's violation of PATBF.

Scenario 1–3

- The likelihood of the violation of PATBF is very high, and, therefore, the likelihood of Obligations 1–4 arising from the violation is also very high. Third States should refrain from acts violating Obligations 1–4 above.
- When the use of force involved in the deployment is grave enough to amount to aggression, the likelihood of Obligation 5 arising would also become high, and third States should also consider what they can do to observe Obligation 5 above.

Scenarios 2–1 and 2–2

- The violation of PATBF is possible, in particular if State B has been aware of State A's administrative measures but has not protested. If there is a possibility that State B has been aware of State A's administrative measures but has not protested, third States should at least take precautionary measures not to violate Obligations 1–4 as much as possible through avoiding explicit recognition of the acquisition of territory through governmental actions directly referring to the territory in question as much as possible.

Scenarios 3–1 and 3–2

- The violation of PATBF is possible, and, therefore, third States should take precautionary measures not to violate Obligations 1–4 above as much as possible through avoiding explicit recognition of the acquisition of territory through governmental actions directly referring to the territory in question.

These obligations cannot substitute for effective actions taken by the Security Council under Chapter VII,[39] and the Security Council should not be allowed to escape its primary responsibility for the maintenance of international peace and security under Article 24 of the UN Charter. At the same time, Member States should also fulfil their duty to cooperate under the 1970 Declaration. It provides:

> The duty of States to co-operate with one another in accordance with the Charter
>
> States have the duty to co-operate with one another, irrespective of the differences in their political, economic and social systems, in the various spheres of international relations, in order to maintain international peace and security …
>
> To this end:
>
> States shall co-operate with other States in the maintenance of international peace and security; …

The Declaration also provides:

> The principle that States shall fulfil in good faith the obligations assumed by them in accordance with the Charter
>
> Every State has the duty to fulfil in good faith the obligations assumed by it in accordance with the Charter of the United Nations.

[39] Korman (1996), pp. 245–248.

> Every State has the duty to fulfil in good faith its obligations under the generally recognized principles and rules of international law. …

While the contents of these obligations remain ambiguous, all the UN Member States must fulfil Obligations 1–5 above in good faith and make efforts to discharge the duty to cooperate with other States in the maintenance of international peace and security.

References

Akehurst, M. (1987). *A Modern Introduction to International Law*, 6th edn. Harper Collins

Bowett, D.W. (1971). International Law Relating to Occupied Territory: A Rejoinder. LQR 87: 473–475

Klein, P. & Koutroulis, V. (2018). Territorial disputes and the use of force, in *Research Handbook on Territorial Disputes in International Law* ed. by Kohen M, Hébié M. Edward Elgar

Brunk, I. & Hakimi, M. (2024). The Prohibition of Annexations and the Foundations of Modern International Law, AJIL 118(3): 417–467

Jennings, R. (1963). *The Acquisition of Territory in International Law*. Manchester University Press

Jennings, R. & Watts, A. (ed.) (1992) *Oppenheim' International Law,* 9th edn. Volume I, Longman

Korman, S. (1996). *The Right of Conquest: The Acquisition of Territory by Force in International Law and Practice,* Clarendon Press Oxford

Mikanagi, T. (2021). Application of the Due Diligence Principle to Cyber Operations. International Law Studies 97: 1019–1038 https://digital-commons.usnwc.edu/cgi/viewcontent.cgi?article=2979&context=ils

O'Meara, C. (2021). *Necessity and Proportionality and the Right of Self-Defence in International Law.* Oxford University Press

Tams, C. (2024). Article 2(4), in *The Charter of the United Nations, A Commentary*, 4th edn. Vol. I, ed. by Simma B et al. Oxford University Press

Chapter 5
Remaining Challenges

5.1 Have We Made Progress in the Past Hundred Years?

More than a hundred years have passed since the League of Nations was established in 1920. Eighty years have passed since the United Nations was established in 1945. Fifty-five years have passed since the Friendly Relations Declaration was adopted in 1970. Having witnessed all the challenges in recent years, we need to ask ourselves: 'Have we made progress in upholding the rule of law against attempts to acquire territory by force in the past hundred years?'

5.1.1 Russian Invasion of Ukraine

The Russian invasion of Ukraine in 2022 has shaken our confidence in the progress which appeared to have been made in the past hundred years. Obviously, how this invasion ends significantly affects the answer to the question above, and we are probably standing at a critical juncture. The rule of law based on international law has not been able to stop the determined attempt by a nuclear power to acquire a neighbouring State's territory by large-scale invasion. On the other hand, more than 140 UN Member States supported GA resolutions condemning this attempt as a violation of PATBF. This global public opinion backed Ukraine's fight against Russian invasion and Ukraine resisted Russia's attempts to establish control over all the territories of the Donetsk, Kherson, Luhansk and Zaporizhzhia regions.

The collective security system of the United Nations under Chapter VII of the UN Charter, where the Security Council has the primary responsibility, did not work in this case due to Russia's veto. This system worked in 1990 when the Security Council adopted resolution 678 against Iraq, but, by design, this system does not work against a P5 State's determined attempts to acquire territory by force.

T. Mikanagi, *Toward Stronger Rule of Law Against Attempts to Acquire Territory by Force*, SpringerBriefs in Law,
https://doi.org/10.1007/978-981-95-2814-1_5

Russia's attempt to acquire territory by force started in 2014 when it attempted to annex Crimea. At that time only 100 Member States supported the GA resolution 68/262, which was a significantly smaller number than the more than 140 that supported GA resolutions on Ukraine in 2022. This difference is at least partly due to the legal ambiguity relating to the situation in Crimea in 2014. Does the non-violent use of armed force amount to prohibited acquisition of territory 'by force'? Does President Putin's apparent recognition of his involvement in sending 'Little Green Men' amount to attribution through adoption under Article 11 of the ILC's Articles on State Responsibility? These questions were not clearly posed and answered at that time. The legal clarity of the situation in February 2022 seemed to have helped in winning more support from UN Member States than in 2014.

5.1.2 Progress in the Clarification of Law and the Role of the ICJ

The UN Charter and the 1970 Declaration have significantly contributed to the clarification of law relating to attempts to acquire territory by force and contributed to the overwhelming support to the GA resolutions on Ukraine in 2022. The application of PATBF to the OPT remained controversial even after the adoption of the 1970 Declaration. However, years of academic debate, discussion in the Security Council and the GA and the two ICJ Advisory Opinions in 2004 and 2024 finally clarified that PATBF applies to the OPT.

Recent years have seen active utilisation of the ICJ by the GA. However, in the history of the ICJ this is a relatively recent phenomenon. In 2019, a project of the Oxford Institute for Law, Ethics and Armed Conflict (ELAC) studied States' willingness to give consent in advance to the compulsory jurisdiction of international courts and tribunals in relation to inter-State disputes. This study resulted in a report titled, 'Prior Consent by States to the Jurisdiction of International Courts and Tribunals in Inter-State Disputes' by Zachary Vermeer and Dapo Akande. This report explains the change in States' attitude toward the ICJ in the post-war period reflected in their acceptance of its jurisdiction. As this report seems to be very informative, it deserves to be quoted at length[1]:

> 41. The International Court of Justice in its early years saw a gradual increase in the number of States accepting jurisdiction under the Optional Clause, from 25 in 1947 to 37 in 1952–53. However, this number declined in the course of the 1950s as a number of States (Bolivia, Brazil, Guatemala and Iran) either terminated their declarations or failed to renew them. In 1955 there were 33 declarations in force, representing just over 40% of the 80 parties to the Statute of the Court. Those States which accepted the Optional Clause were largely drawn from the Western bloc in Europe and the Americas, with the addition of a few non-aligned States like India. In contrast, no States from the Socialist bloc accepted the ICJ's jurisdiction under the Optional Clause.

[1] Vermeer and Akande (2019), pp. 18–20.

42. The subsequent years saw a significant fall in the percentage of States accepting the Optional Clause. While the absolute number of declarations in force increased somewhat, this did not keep pace with the rapid increase in UN membership (and hence parties to the Statute) resulting from decolonization. By 1979 45 States had Optional Clause declarations in force out of a total of 155 parties to the Statute (29.0%). In addition to the continued abstention of the Socialist bloc, this reflected the fact that relatively few of the newly independent States accepted the Court's compulsory jurisdiction. In part this reflected the understandable wariness of these States concerning restrictions on their recently obtained sovereignty. It has also been attributed to the alienation of the developing world from the Court following its 1966 decision in the *South West Africa* case, which gave rise to a widespread view that the Court's approach to international law reflected the interests of Western powers.[2]

43. Since then however the percentage of States making Optional Clause declarations has seen a steady increase. This shift is sometimes said to date back to the Court's decision in the Nicaragua case, where it demonstrated its willingness to find in favour of Nicaragua and against the United States in a highly sensitive political context. Although this decision resulted in the United States' termination of its Optional Clause declaration, it may have increased the prestige of the Court in the eyes of smaller and/or developing States who make up the majority of the international community. It was around this time that the number of cases brought to the Court, which had fallen to a very low number in the 1970s, began to increase again. Significant growth in the percentage of States making Optional Clause declarations however did not occur until some years later. In 1993 the number of States with Optional Clause declarations in force was 56 out of 186 parties to the Statute, or 30.1%, little more than the 29.0% of States in 1980. By 2009 however the number had increased to 67 out of 192 UN members, or 34.9%. This trend has continued in the past decade, so that there are currently 74 States with declarations in force out of 193 UN members, or 38.3%.

Currently, there are only 74 out of 193 UN Member States accepting the ICJ's jurisdiction through their declarations under Article 36 of the ICJ Statute. To some extent, this number of States accepting the ICJ's jurisdiction through this declaration reflects the weakness of the rule of law at the international level. However, the improvement in the developing States' perception of the ICJ in the post-war period mentioned in the report above is a positive sign of improvement in the strength of the rule of law among nations.

Developing countries have been utilising the ICJ in resolving the territorial dispute between themselves. In this book, I have mentioned the ICJ cases between Indonesia and Malaysia, Malaysia and Singapore, Cameroon and Nigeria, and Costa Rica and Nicaragua. I have also mentioned the Eritrea–Ethiopia Claims Commission (EECC). Some of these cases involved the deployment of armed forces to disputed territories, but through the third-party dispute settlement mechanisms, they resolved the disputes based on international law. These examples indicate important progress we have seen in the past hundred years in strengthening the rule of law against attempts to acquire territory by force.

Judgments and awards made in these cases have also contributed to the clarification of international law relating to attempts to acquire territory by force. Furthermore, Advisory Opinions, in particular the 2024 ICJ Advisory Opinion, significantly contributed to the clarification of the nature and effect of PATBF.

---

[2] Crawford (2017), p. 97. Moyn and Özsu (2020), p. 38.

5.1.3 *Reasons Behind the Unwillingness to Accept the ICJ's Jurisdiction*

On the other hand, among the P5, only the UK has been maintaining the declaration under Article 36(2) of the ICJ Statute. A State accepting the ICJ's jurisdiction over relevant legal issues is less likely to resort to forcible measures which are difficult to justify under international law than a State not doing so. Therefore, the acceptance of the ICJ's legally binding dispute settlement mechanism works as a deterrent against unlawful forcible measures and contributes to the maintenance of international peace and security. On the other hand, as pointed out in Sect. 3.3.4 above, if a State resorts to forcible measures difficult to justify under international law and offers negotiation as the only means of settlement and rejects a legally binding dispute settlement, that State cannot claim to be a faithful observer of international law.

As pointed out in Sect. 2.1.3 above, during the inter-war period, some States were not satisfied with the existing territorial *status quo,* and major powers did not give up their own interests for the effectiveness of the collective security mechanism for the maintenance of international peace and security. Thus, there was an inherent difficulty in upholding the rule of law against attempts to acquire territory by force. In 1970 the dissatisfaction about the territorial *status quo* seemed to have eased to some extent, but some major powers continued to hesitate to give up their own interests for international peace and security and the post-Cold War development left Russia dissatisfied with the current territorial *status quo*. However, as pointed out in Sect. 2.2.2.1, the changes in the territorial situations in the former Soviet Union were not made through use of force, and, if there is any dissatisfaction about territorial changes brought about without use of force after 1970, it would not justify deviation from PATBF which was accepted in 1970.

In an article published in 2002 titled 'Power and Weakness', Robert Kagan provided a useful explanation about the relationship between international law and power. This article was written in an international environment different from now, but it still gives us an interesting perspective. Kagan wrote rather bluntly: 'Americans generally favour policies of coercion rather than persuasion … They are less inclined to act through international institutions such as the United Nations, less inclined to work cooperatively with other nations to pursue common goals, more sceptical about international law, and more willing to operate outside its strictures when they deem it necessary, or even merely useful'.[3] He explained this inclination based on the power equation. According to him: 'When the United States was weak, it practiced the strategies of indirection, the strategies of weakness; now that the United States is powerful, it behaves as powerful nations do. When the European great powers were strong, they believed in strength and martial glory'. In short, Kagen was saying that powerful States have less incentive to observe international law than weaker States. Morgenthau also wrote in 'Politics Among Nations – The Struggle

[3] Kagan (2002), para. 3.

for Power and Peace' that 'any system of existing law is of necessity an ally of the status quo' and concluded as follows: 'Imperialistic nations are inevitably opposed to the existing status quo and its legal order and will not think of submitting the controversy to the authoritative decision of an international court. For the court cannot grant their demands without destroying the very foundation on which its authority rests'.[4]

In the post-war history, the US has not resorted to use of force to acquire territory in violation of PATBF. However, if a State, which is protected by veto power, considers itself to be militarily or otherwise powerful enough to deter other States from resorting to the right to collective self-defence in helping the victim State and if it also believes it is economically resilient enough to survive difficulties caused by measures taken by other States to stop the powerful State, international law cannot effectively prevent it from attempting to change the territorial *status quo* by use of force.

5.2 What Can We Do Now?

5.2.1 Available Options

If so, does it mean that we must accept that the rule of law does not work against a determined attempt by a P5 State to acquire territory by force? We should answer: 'Not necessarily'. In this book I have been trying to emphasise the importance of pressure exerted by third States. If an overwhelming majority of States condemn the deployment of armed forces to acquire territory as a violation of PATBF, or PUF, and continue to refrain from recognising the territory as the deploying State's territory, in the longer term these actions can exert unignorable pressure on the deploying State. If States recognise the obligations for third States mentioned in Sect. 4.2 above, extending not only to obligation not to recognise, but also to obligation not to render assistance and even to obligation to cooperate, the pressure exerted by third States will become stronger.

In addition, the rejection of the ICJ's jurisdiction by the deploying State is likely to show its legal weakness. If the State does not care about international law at all, arguments based on international law will not work; but, if the State is claiming to be acting in accordance with international law, there might be a way to undermine its claim. For example, if a P5 State invades a non-P5 neighbour's internationally recognised territory by large-scale use of armed force, unilaterally conducts a 'referendum' in areas under its military occupation, declares their annexation, and attempts to justify it by right to self-defence, the invaded non-P5 State should call on the invading P5 State to bring the issue of the legality of the latter's attempted annexation to the ICJ. If the invading State consents to bringing the case before the

[4] Morgenthau (1985), p. 465.

ICJ, the ICJ will most certainly determine that the attempted annexation amounts to a violation of PATBF. If the invading State rejects this proposal, the invaded State may be able to show that the invading State is avoiding the ICJ on the issue relating to PATBF because it knows the weakness of its legal justification. The invaded State can also achieve a similar effect through making a declaration under Article 36(2) of the ICJ Statute.

There might be other options to uphold the rule of law against attempts to acquire territory by force, and we need to make efforts to look for such options. Kennan famously wrote in his 'American Diplomacy': 'instead of making ourselves slaves of the concepts of international law and morality, we would confine these concepts to the unobtrusive, almost feminine, function of the gentle civilizer of national self-interest in which they find their true value'.[5] Even if the current weak system of international law cannot effectively stop attempts to acquire territory by force, by using international law as a 'gentle civilizer' of the behaviour of States, including through putting pressure by not recognising, not assisting and preventing assistance, and through showing to the world the weakness of the deploying State's legal justification, the rule of law may be able to retain its minimum force to encourage the observance of international law. Brierly also famously wrote in his 'Law of Nations' in 1928 as follows:[6]

> … the law of nations is neither a chimera nor panacea, but just one institution among others which we have at our disposal for the building up of a saner international order. It is foolish to underestimate either the services that it is rendering to-day, or the need for its improvement and extension.

In the Pact for the Future,[7] which was quoted in Sects. 1.2 and 3.3.4 above, UN Member States reaffirmed 'the imperative of upholding and promoting the rule of law at the international level in accordance with the principles of the Charter of the United Nations', and in this regard, they recalled the importance of the 1970 Friendly Relations Declaration. In its Action 17, Member States also stated that '[w]e recognize the positive contribution of the International Court of Justice, the principal judicial organ of the United Nations, including in adjudicating disputes among States'. These words should be faithfully observed by the Member States.

5.2.2 Conclusion: The Role of International Lawyers

Let me conclude this small book by emphasising the importance of international lawyers in upholding the rule of law against attempts to acquire territory by force. Here, the term 'international lawyers' means experts on public international law both in academia and in practice, including law firms and governments.

---

[5] Kennan (1951), p. 50

[6] Clapham (2012), Preface to the First Edition (by Brierly).

[7] UN Doc. A/RES/79/1.

While I was Japanese Legal Advisor, with the assistance of colleagues and partners, I worked for the creation of a seminar called 'Tokyo International Law Seminar (TILS)'. The first TILS took place at the United Nations University in Tokyo in August 2023, and it is now taking place every summer.[8] TILS is a training program organised by the MOFA that provides lectures in the field of international law for officials and legal experts from Asia and Africa. Through the exchanges among the participants, the seminar aims to enhance knowledge of international law and contribute to peace guided by the rule of law. In the inaugural lecture of TILS 2023, I talked about the importance of the rule of law among nations for peace and the importance of the role of international lawyers as 'stabilisers' of international relations.

International lawyers tend to have similar academic backgrounds in studying international law at universities reading similar textbooks and articles.[9] As a result, they share common knowledge of international law, including the knowledge on the provisions of relevant treaties, the ICJ and other jurisprudence, and essential reference materials like the ILC reports. Despite occasional differences in political positions among governments, international lawyers' advice to policy makers is often based on the common knowledge of international law. In my view, this should provide a mutually understandable basis for communication among governments that can establish international relations based on international law. In other words, international law should play the role of common language through which different governments can communicate, ideally, even in the time of confrontation, and international lawyers can play the role of interlocutors speaking the same language of international law.

My argument for the 'stabilising' role of international lawyers is premised upon two preconditions.

First, international lawyers working for the governments must have sound and updated knowledge about the current state of international law. International lawyers working for the government need to continue efforts throughout their career. In a sense, international lawyers' lives are like those of monks going through austerities at temples. One must be rather stoic in self-imposing the task of reading lengthy judgments and documents, sometimes in hundreds of pages, to maintain an updated knowledge of international law.

Second, international lawyers must maintain good working relationships with the policy side. Without a good working relationship with the policy side, legal advisors cannot effectively contribute to the policy-making process. This is probably the most fundamental problem commonly experienced by legal departments in the governments. Sometimes, legal advisors' offices are not involved in the policy-making process at a sufficiently early stage, and they find it very difficult to catch up and effectively contribute to the decision making on issues involving legal questions. In some cases, an apparent contradiction between policy preference and legal

[8] https://www.mofa.go.jp/policy/inter_law/law/pagewe_000001_00043.html

[9] Lowe (2007), p. 22.

considerations could emerge. However, for the policy makers it is useful to obtain the moral high ground through making legally sound arguments. Therefore, it is essential for international lawyers to maintain good working relationships with the policy side.

If these two conditions are met, legal advisors can advise policy makers to take legally sound positions and, thus, contribute to the stabilisation of international relations based on international law. This stabilising role of international lawyers can be strengthened through human networking among international lawyers from various countries and regions. If the international lawyers working for different governments know each other and can communicate with each other, that can provide a kind of safety net. Amid political and diplomatic tension, it would be difficult to communicate among lawyers, but the knowledge of the positions taken by international lawyers advising the other side might give some insight into the options to be considered by the opposite number, which should lead to more effective legal advice.

In addition, if a new situation involving questions relating to international law emerges in international relations and there is a need for finding like-minded partners in addressing the situation, the network of international lawyers can also help cooperation with potential partners. The 1970 Declaration declared that Member States have a duty to cooperate in order to maintain international peace and security, and the preamble of the 1970 Declaration also says that the UN Charter is of paramount importance in the promotion of the rule of law among nations, and that the faithful observance of the principles in the Declaration, which include PATBF, is of the greatest importance for the maintenance of international peace and security. These pronouncements remind international lawyers that they have a duty to cooperate for the faithful observance of these principles and, when faced with their serious violation, international lawyers have a collective duty to cooperate against the violation.

References

Clapham, A. (2012). *Brierly's Law of Nations*, 7th edn. Oxford University Press

Crawford, J. (2017). The Place of the International Court in International Dispute Settlement', in *The International Legal Order: Current Needs and Possible Responses*, ed. by Crawford J, Koroma A, Mahmoudi S, Pellet A, Brill

Kagan, R. (2002). Power and Weakness, Policy Review, Hoover Institution, Stanford University https://www.hoover.org/research/power-and-weakness

Kennan, G. (1951). *American Diplomacy 1900–1950*, The University of Chicago Press (reissued in 2012)

Lowe, V. (2007). *International Law*. Oxford University Press

Morgenthau, H. (1985). *Politics Among Nations – The Struggle for Power and Peace*, 6th edn. McGraw-Hill

Moyn, S. & Özsu, U. (2020). The Historical Origins and Setting of the Friendly Relations Declaration, in *The UN Friendly Relations Declaration at 50*, ed. by Viñuales, Cambridge University Press

Vermeer, Z. & Akande, D. (2019). Prior Consent by States to the Jurisdiction of International Courts and Tribunals in Inter-State Disputes. https://www.elac.ox.ac.uk/wp-content/uploads/2023/10/PriorConsent_Final_Report.pdf

Index

T. Mikanagi, *Toward Stronger Rule of Law Against Attempts to Acquire Territory by Force*, SpringerBriefs in Law,
https://doi.org/10.1007/978-981-95-2814-1

MIX
Papier aus verantwortungsvollen Quellen
Paper from responsible sources
FSC® C105338

If you have any concerns about our products,
you can contact us on
ProductSafety@springernature.com

In case Publisher is established outside the EU,
the EU authorized representative is:
Springer Nature Customer Service Center GmbH
Europaplatz 3, 69115 Heidelberg, Germany

Printed by Libri Plureos GmbH
in Hamburg, Germany